VOCA EDGE

S·M·A·R·T

STORYTELLING VOCABULARY

Level
5

We're

Introduction

Every student knows acquiring English vocabulary is a basic necessity for learning the English language. However, not many are aware that simply memorizing vocabulary words is not enough. In order to master a language, students need to spend more time learning how to use these words and what they really mean. Yet, students still spend countless hours memorizing rather than learning.

Even worse is the fact that most vocabulary books are extremely difficult and boring. Fortunately, there is a way for everyone to change their perspective on learning vocabulary. Now you can develop your vocabulary in an enjoyable way. The VOCA EDGE SMART series will help you simultaneously enlarge your vocabulary and improve your English.

This series uses an integrated approach to learning English. Listening, reading, writing and comprehension are all covered in this series.

One of the key features of this series is that it revolves around the daily lives of several characters and the challenges they face in growing up. By reading each episode, students will learn the natural and functional use of English vocabulary.

Each level of this series comes with one textbook and one audio component. Each book is organized into 6 chapters, each of which consists of 2-4 related units. Each book also deals with a variety of unique and interesting topics, and the series is graded to an appropriate length and depth to suit the needs of students with varying levels of English proficiency.

After studying each unit, students will be challenged to review the words and expressions they learned through a series of related questions and activities. Students can listen to the entire script in MP3 format. We invite you to let this series help you take the next step in your journey towards becoming a more proficient speaker of English. We are confident that the VOCA EDGE SMART series can help you make a dramatic improvement in your English ability.

Contents

책의 구성과 특징

1단계

- Preview 단계로, 주어진 삽화를 보고 각 Unit의 에피소드를 먼저 추측해볼 수 있습니다.

2단계

- 일기, 대화, 편지 등의 다양한 형태로 제공된 10대의 일상 생활 속 에피소드를 눈으로 읽고 귀로 듣는 단계로, 어휘뿐만 아니라 Reading 및 Listening, Conversation 학습 효과까지 누릴 수 있습니다.

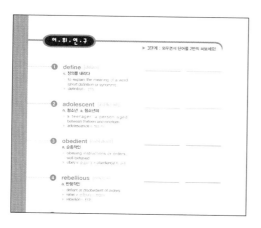

3단계

- 앞의 지문에서 가장 중요한 어휘만을 골라 익히고 연습하는 단계로, 각 단어와 관련된 유의어 및 반의어, 파생어를 함께 학습할 수 있습니다.

Exercise

- 중요한 단어 및 표현들을 빈칸에 채워 넣으며, 앞에서 배운 어휘들을 다시 확인하고 점검할 수 있습니다.

Dictation

- CD를 듣고 빈칸에 해당하는 단어를 채워 넣으며, Unit의 전체 내용을 복습할 수 있습니다. 또한, 자신의 약점을 파악하여 취약부분만을 집중적으로 학습할 수 있습니다.

Review Test

- 각 챕터가 끝나면 앞에서 배운 중요한 단어 30개를 듣고 받아씀으로써, 정확한 발음 공부와 함께 단어 복습도 함께 할 수 있습니다.

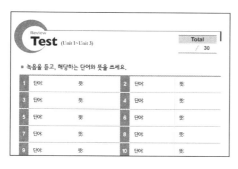

Voca Plus

- 영단어들이 어떻게 구성되어 있는지에 대해 어원을 포함한 기본적인 정보들을 배우며, 각 챕터와 관련된 문화 정보와 필수 어휘들도 함께 익힐 수 있습니다.

SMART **L**evel.5

Chapter 1

Teen Life

Chapter 1
Teen Life

▶ 1단계 : 먼저 그림을 보고, 이 장의 에피소드를 추측해 보세요.

→ **freeze while waiting for favorite stars** ●

● **imitate the hairstyles of favorite stars** ←

→ **pretend to concentrate on one's studies** ●

● **squeeze pimples** ←

Dear Mom,

How can you define teenagers? ● Mom, what were you like when you were an adolescent? ● Were you obedient? ● Were you rebellious? ● What do you think typical teens are like? ● I'm talking about ordinary teens like me. ● Teens are energetic. ● We don't mind freezing while waiting outside for our favorite stars.

We like to imitate the hairstyles of our favorite stars. ● We want our privacy. ● We don't like to have our privacy interrupted. ● We have our own individual phones. ● We like decorating our phones with stickers. ● Mom, I know you chat on the phone. ● We prefer to text on the phone. ● We post images of celebrities on our blogs. ● We even put anonymous messages on the Internet. ● Sometimes harsh comments can cause problems, though. ● Now, more teens are eager to have their own blog.

Some blogs provide practical tips. ● They even help us keep up with fashions that are in vogue. ● Some tips are about effective study habits. ● Tips like how to pretend to concentrate on our studies while sending text messages. ● Do you know what we like to do when we feel stressed? ● We're reluctant to spend time on schoolwork and prefer to hang out with friends. ● We like to have big feasts of dukbokki and kimbab. ● We often stand in front of the mirror squeezing pimples on our faces. ● Mom, when you were a teenager, were you like me?

1 define [difáin]

v. 정의를 내리다

▶ to explain the meaning of a word (short definition or synonym)
▶ definition n. 정의

_____ _____

2 adolescent [ædɔlésənt]

n. 청소년 a. 청소년의

▶ a teenager, a person aged between thirteen and nineteen
▶ adolescence n. 청소년기

_____ _____

3 obedient [oʊbíːdiənt]

a. 순종적인

▶ obeying instructions or orders, well-behaved
▶ obey v. 순종하다 ▶ obedience n. 순종

_____ _____

4 rebellious [ribéljəs]

a. 반항적인

▶ defiant or disobedient of orders
▶ rebel v. 반항하다 n. 반항아
▶ rebellion n. 반항

_____ _____

5 typical [típikəl]

▶ normal, ordinary, usual, average
▶ type n. 전형

_____ _____

6 ordinary [ɔ́ːrdənèri]

a. 일반적인

▶ normal, common, not special

_____ _____

7 energetic [ènərdʒétik]

a. 활기가 넘치는

▶ having a lot of energy, being very active
▶ energy n. 기운, 에너지

_____ _____

⑧ freeze [friːz]
v. 얼다, 얼리다
▶ to become ice or become covered in ice
▶ freezing a. 어는
▶ frozen a. 냉동된

_____ _____

⑨ imitate [ímitèit]
v. 모방하다
▶ to follow the style of someone or something else
▶ imitation n. 모방

_____ _____

⑩ privacy [práivəsi]
n. 사생활
▶ the state of spending time alone
▶ private a. 사적인

_____ _____

⑪ interrupt [ìntərʌ́pt]
v. 방해하다
▶ to temporarily stop a person from doing something
▶ interruption n. 방해

_____ _____

⑫ individual [ìndəvídʒuəl]
a. 개인적인 n. 개인
▶ personal, belonging to one person
▶ individually ad. 개별적으로

_____ _____

⑬ decorate [dékərèit]
v. 장식하다
▶ to make something more attractive by adding things to it
▶ decoration n. 장식
▶ decorative a. 장식의

_____ _____

⑭ chat [tʃǽt]
v. 수다를 떨다 n. 잡담
▶ to talk to each other in an informal and friendly way

_____ _____

15 **prefer** [prifə́:r]

v. 선호하다, 더 좋아하다

▶ to like one thing more than another

▶ preference n. 선호

_____ _____

16 **celebrity** [səlébrəti]

n. 유명인사

▶ a famous person

_____ _____

17 **anonymous** [ənánəməs]

a. 익명의

▶ without giving one's name, unidentified

▶ anonymity n. 익명, 작자 불명

_____ _____

18 **harsh** [hɑːrʃ]

a. 무자비한, 심한

▶ unkind, cruel

_____ _____

19 **eager** [íːgər]

a. 열망하는

▶ having a desire to do something

▶ eagerness n. 열망, 갈망

▶ be eager to+ V ~하는 것을 좋아하다

_____ _____

20 **provide** [prəváid]

v. 제공하다, 주다

▶ to give something to a person

▶ provider n. 공급자

_____ _____

21 **vogue** [voug]

n. 유행, 유행하는 것 a. 유행의

▶ a thing that is popular for a short time

▶ in vogue 유행하는

_____ _____

▶ 외우면서 단어를 2번씩 써보세요!

22 effective [iféktiv]
a. 효과적인
▶ productive, producing a good result
▶ effect n. 효과
▶ effectively ad. 효과적으로

_____   _____

23 concentrate [kánsəntrèit]
v. 집중하다
▶ to focus on something
▶ concentration n. 집중
▶ concentrate on ~에 집중하다

_____   _____

24 stressed [strést]
a. 스트레스가 쌓인
▶ anxious and tense
▶ stress v. 강조하다, 괴롭히다 n. 스트레스

_____   _____

23 reluctant [rilʌ́ktənt]
a. 망설이는
▶ unwilling to do something
▶ reluctance n. 망설임
▶ be reluctant to+ V ~하는 것을 망설이다

_____   _____

24 feast [fiːst]
n. 진수성찬, 잔치
▶ a large and special meal

_____   _____

25 squeeze [skwiːz]
v. 쥐어짜다
▶ to press something firmly from several sides

_____   _____

Exercise

A 주어진 뜻에 해당하는 단어를 보기에서 찾아 쓰세요.

| adolescent | feast | typical | prefer | decorate |
| interrupt | anonymous | vogue | eager | imitate |

① a teenager, a person aged between thirteen and nineteen   _____
② having a desire to do something   _____
③ without giving one's name, unidentified   _____
④ a large and special meal   _____
⑤ to like one thing more than another   _____
⑥ a thing that is popular for a short time   _____
⑦ normal, ordinary, usual, average   _____
⑧ to follow the style of someone or something else   _____
⑨ to make something more attractive by adding things to it   _____
⑩ to temporarily stop a person from doing something   _____

B 단어의 관계에 맞게 빈칸을 채우세요.

① rebellious : _____ = 반항적인 : 반항
② effective : effect = _____ : 효과
③ _____ : definition = 정의하다 : 정의
④ reluctant : _____ = 망설이는 : 망설임
⑤ freeze : _____ = 얼다 : 냉동된
⑥ _____ : energy = 활기 넘치는 : 기운
⑦ provide : provider = 제공하다 : _____
⑧ obedient : _____ = 순종적인 : 순종하다

C 의미가 같도록 알맞은 단어를 넣어 문장을 완성하세요.

1. We want our _____.
   우리는 우리만의 사생활을 원해요.

2. We have our own _____ phones.
   우리는 개인 전화를 가지고 있어요.

3. Sometimes _____ comments can cause problems, though.
   때로는 무자비한 비판이 문제가 되기도 하지만요.

4. I'm talking about _____ teens like me.
   저와 같은 일반적인 십대에 대해 이야기하는 거예요.

5. We post images of _____ on our blogs.
   우리는 유명인의 이미지를 블로그에 올려요.

6. We often stand in front of the mirror _____ pimples on our faces.
   우리는 얼굴에 난 여드름을 짜면서 종종 거울 앞에 서 있죠.

7. Do you know what we like to do when we feel _____?
   우리가 스트레스를 받을 때 무엇을 하고 싶어하는지 아세요?

8. Tips like how to pretend to _____ on our studies while sending text messages.
   문자 메시지를 보내면서 공부에 집중하는 척하는 방법과 같은 조언이죠.

D 녹음된 내용을 듣고, 다음 빈칸에 들어갈 단어나 표현을 쓰세요.

Dear Mom,

How can you _____ define teenagers? ● Mom, what were you like when you were an adolescent _____ ? ● Were you obedient _____ ? ● Were you rebellious _____ ? ● What do you think _____ teens are like? ● I'm talking about _____ teens like me. ● Teens are energetic _____. ● We don't mind _____ while waiting outside for our favorite stars.

We like to _____ the hairstyles of our favorite stars. ● We want our _____. ● We don't like to have our privacy _____. ● We have our own _____ phones. ● We like _____ our phones with stickers.

● Mom, I know you _____ on the phone. ● We _____ to text on the phone. ● We post images of _____ on our blogs. ● We even put _____ messages on the Internet. ● Sometimes _____ comments can cause problems, though. ● Now, more teens are _____ to have their own blog.

Some blogs _____ practical tips. ● They even help us keep up with fashions that are in _____. ● Some tips are about _____ study habits. ● Tips like how to pretend to _____ on our studies while sending text messages. ● Do you know what we like to do when we feel _____? ● We're _____ to spend time on schoolwork and prefer to hang out with friends. ● We like to have big _____ of dukbokki and kimbab. ● We often stand in front of the mirror _____ pimples on our faces. ● Mom, when you were a teenager, were you like me?

▶ 1단계 : 먼저 그림을 보고, 이 장의 에피소드를 추측해 보세요.

→ **persist listening to music**

→ **force someone to give something**

Episode

▶ 2단계 : 녹음 내용을 들으며, 추측한 에피소드와 비교해 보세요.

When do you feel frustrated? ● Is it when you get poor grades on your report card? ● How about when you feel isolated from friends? ● I've had successive bad luck. ● It reminds me of a proverb that it never rains but it pours. ● In the morning, I had a big argument with my mom. ● She compelled me to put my pajamas back in the closet. ● I refused to do it. ● I covered my ears and persisted listening to my music. ● Mom was furious with me. ● She said I misbehaved. ● I slammed the door hard and left home. ● I got on the bus and inside the bus it was stuffy because of the poor ventilation. ● Later I regretted my behavior. ● I felt uneasy.

During class, my cell phone vibrated. ● My teacher forced me to give it to him. ● Then the teacher announced to the whole class that he would keep it for one month. ● I couldn't use my transportation pass. ● It was attached to the cell phone, so I had to walk home temporarily. ● I was supposed to see my friends, but we had to cancel our plans because I couldn't contact them. ● Now, I realize how indispensible my cell phone is. ● At home, my mom told me to apologize to my teacher. ● I guess I'd better listen to my mom's advice.

▶ 3단계 : 외우면서 단어를 2번씩 써보세요!

1 **frustrated** [frÁstreitid]
a. 좌절감을 느낀, 실망한
  ▶ disappointed, discouraged
  ▶ frustrate v. 좌절(실망)시키다
  ▶ frustration n. 좌절, 실망

_____ _____

2 **report card** [ripɔ́ːrt kɑːrd]
성적표
  ▶ a document that records one's grades

_____ _____

3 **isolated** [áisəlèitid]
a. 고립된
  ▶ being separated from other people
  ▶ isolate v. 고립(격리)시키다
  ▶ isolation n. 고립

_____ _____

4 **successive** [səksésiv]
a. 연속하는
  ▶ happening one after another

_____ _____

5 **proverb** [právəːrb]
n. 속담
  ▶ a well-known sentence that often gives advice

_____ _____

6 **pour** [pɔːr]
v. 억수같이 퍼붓다
  ▶ to flow quickly, to empty a large amount of liquid

_____ _____

7 **argument** [áːrgjəmənt]
n. 말다툼
  ▶ a disagreement with another person
  ▶ argue v. 말다툼하다

_____ _____

▶ 외우면서 단어를 2번씩 써보세요!

8 **compel** [kὰmpəl]
v. 강요하다
▶ to force or make someone do something

_____   _____

9 **refuse** [rifjúːz]
v. 거절하다
▶ to say no, to choose not to do something
▶ refusal n. 거절

_____   _____

10 **persist** [pəːrsíst]
v. 지속하다
▶ to continue to do something
▶ persistence n. 지속성, 끈기
▶ persistent a. 지속적인

_____   _____

11 **furious** [fjúəriəs]
a. 격노한
▶ extremely angry
▶ fury n. 격노

_____   _____

12 **misbehave** [mìsbihéiv]
v. 못되게 굴다, 버릇 없이 행동하다
▶ to behave badly
▶ misbehavior n. 버릇없음

_____   _____

13 **slam** [slǽm]
v. (문 등을) 세게 닫다
▶ to shut something e.g. the door noisily

_____   _____

14 **ventilation** [véntəlèiʃən]
n. 환기
▶ a state of allowing fresh air to get inside
▶ ventilate v. 환기시키다

_____   _____

⑮ regret [rigrét]
v. 후회하다 n. 후회
▶ to feel sorry about something someone has done
▶ regretful a. 후회하는
▶ regrettable a. 유감스러운

_____ _____

⑯ uneasy [ʌníːzi]
a. 불편한
▶ uncomfortable

_____ _____

⑰ vibrate [váibreit]
v. 진동하다
▶ to shake or fluctuate
▶ vibration n. 진동

_____ _____

⑱ force [fɔːrs]
v. 강요하다
▶ to compel or make someone do something.

_____ _____

⑲ announce [ənáuns]
v. 알리다
▶ to tell several or many people about something
▶ announcement n. 공표

_____ _____

⑳ transportation
[trænspərtéiʃn]
n. 교통
▶ any type of vehicle used to travel from one place to another

_____ _____

㉑ attach [ətǽtʃ]
v. 달다, 첨부하다
▶ to connect or stick one thing onto another
▶ attachment n. 부착

_____ _____

▶ 외우면서 단어를 2번씩 써보세요!

22 temporarily [témpərərili]
ad. 일시적으로
▶ for a short time, not permanently

_____   _____

23 suppose [səpóuz]
v. ~하기로 하다, 추정하다
▶ to intend to do something
▶ be supposed to + V ~하기로 되어 있다

_____   _____

24 cancel [kǽnsəl]
v. 취소하다
▶ not to do something that someone planned to do
▶ cancellation n. 취소

_____   _____

25 contact [kántækt]
v. 연락하다 n. 연락
▶ to speak or write to someone

_____   _____

26 indispensable [ìndispènsəbl]
a. 필수적인, 없어서는 안 될
▶ essential, absolutely necessary

_____   _____

27 apologize [əpálədʒàiz]
v. 사과하다
▶ to say sorry
▶ apology n. 사과

_____   _____

28 advice [ədváis]
n. 충고
▶ a helpful suggestion
▶ advise v. 충고하다

_____   _____

Exercise

A 주어진 뜻에 해당하는 단어를 보기에서 찾아 쓰세요.

> report card   pour compel   proverb   successive
> misbehave   transportation   slam   ventilation   uneasy

① a document that records one's grades   _____
② happening one after another   _____
③ a well-known sentence that often gives advice   _____
④ to flow quickly, to empty a large amount of liquid   _____
⑤ to force or make someone do something   _____
⑥ to behave badly   _____
⑦ to shut something e.g. the door noisily   _____
⑧ a state of allowing fresh air to get inside   _____
⑨ uncomfortable   _____
⑩ any type of vehicle used to travel from one place to another _____

B 단어의 관계에 맞게 빈칸을 채우세요.

① advise : _____ = 충고하다 : 충고
② apologize : _____ = 사과하다 : 사과
③ _____ : vibration = 진동하다 : 진동
④ attach : attachment = 첨부하다 : _____
⑤ _____ : fury = 격노한 : 격노
⑥ refuse : _____ = 거절하다 : 거절
⑦ isolated : _____ = 고립된 : 고립
⑧ _____ : argument = 말다툼하다 : 말다툼

C 의미가 같도록 알맞은 단어를 넣어 문장을 완성하세요.

1. Is it when you get poor grades on your _____?
   성적표에 점수가 좋지 않을 때인가요?

2. When do you feel _____?
   당신은 언제 좌절감을 느끼나요?

3. I've had _____ bad luck.
   저는 불행이 연속적으로 닥친 적이 있어요.

4. I covered my ears and _____ listening to my music.
   저는 귀를 막고 음악을 계속 들었어요.

5. Later I _____ my behavior.
   나중에 저는 제 행동을 후회했어요.

6. I got on the bus and inside the bus it was stuffy because of the poor _____.
   저는 버스를 탔고 버스 안에는 환기가 잘 안되어서 공기가 탁했어요.

7. I couldn't use my _____ pass.
   저는 교통카드를 쓸 수 없었어요.

8. Now, I realize how _____ my cell phone is.
   이제는 제 휴대 전화가 얼마나 필수적인지 알게 되었어요.

D 녹음된 내용을 듣고, 다음 빈칸에 들어갈 단어나 표현을 쓰세요.

When do you feel _____? ● Is it when you get poor grades on your _____ _____? ● How about when you feel _____ from friends? ● I've had _____ bad luck. ● It reminds me of a _____ that it never rains but it _____. ● In the morning, I had a big _____ with my mom. ● She _____ me to put my pajamas back in the closet. ● I _____ to do it. ● I covered my ears and _____ listening to my music. ● Mom was _____ with me. ● She said I _____. ● I _____ the door hard and left home. ● I got on the bus and inside the bus it was stuffy because of the poor _____. ● Later I _____ my behavior. ● I felt _____.

During class, my cell phone _____. ● My teacher _____ me to give it to him. ● Then the teacher _____ to the whole class that he would keep it for one month. ● I couldn't use my _____ pass. ● It was _____ to the cell phone, so I had to walk home _____. ● I was _____ to see my friends, but we had to _____ our plans because I couldn't _____ them. ● Now, I realize how _____ my cell phone is. ● At home, my mom told me to _____ to my teacher. ● I guess I'd better listen to my mom's _____.

▶ 1단계 : 먼저 그림을 보고, 이 장의 에피소드를 추측해 보세요.

→ be identical

balance on a board ←

→ express one's condolences

Dear Brownie,

Goodbye, Brownie. I'm sure you're in heaven. ● Brownie, you were such a good companion to Sara and me. ● I remember how graciousyou were. ● We dyed your hair purple. ● You were athletic. ● You could balance on a board. ● You liked tuna when you were pregnant. ● Last month your three puppies were born. ● They are so adorable. ● Do you know the puppies are identical?

They resemble you. ● Your puppies are a blessing to us. ● They are all pure-bred like you. ● We were shocked at the news that you had terminal cancer. ● Sara told me that you were taken to the intensive care unit. ● I heard the heartbreaking news. ● This morning we all mourned. ● Sara said there would be a funeral. ● I read an elegy. ● Sara wept all day. ● She was in despair. ● I sympathized with her feelings.

I tried to comfort Sara. ● It was unbearable for her. ● Other friends expressed their condolences. ● We unanimously agreed to bury you. ● We put a grave stone above you with these words – Goodbye, Brownie. ● You will stay immortal in our memories.

▶ 3단계 : 외우면서 단어를 2번씩 써보세요!

1 **heaven** [hévən]
n. 천국
▶ the place where God and angels live and where Christians believe they go after they die
▶ heavenly a. 천국 같은, 하늘의

_____ _____

2 **companion** [kəmpǽnjən]
n. 친구
▶ a person whom someone spends time with
▶ companionship n. 교제
▶ company n. 동료

_____ _____

3 **gracious** [gréiʃəs]
a. 상냥한
▶ well-mannered, polite
▶ grace n. 고상함, 은혜

_____ _____

4 **dye** [dai]
v. 염색하다
▶ to change one's hair color

_____ _____

5 **athletic** [æθlétik]
a. 운동 신경이 있는
▶ strong and healthy, full of life and energy
▶ athlete n. 운동선수

_____ _____

6 **balance** [bǽləns]
v. 균형을 잡다 n. 균형
▶ to be steady and not fall off

_____ _____

7 **pregnant** [prégnənt]
a. 임신한
▶ having a baby inside one's body
▶ pregnancy n. 임신

_____ _____

▶ 외우면서 단어를 2번씩 써보세요!

8 bear [bɛər]
v. 낳다
▶ to give birth to a child
▷ birth n. 출생
▷ be born 태어나다

_____ _____

9 adorable [ədɔ́:rəbəl]
a. 귀여운
▶ cute, attractive
▷ adore v. 아주 좋아하다

_____ _____

10 identical [aidéntikəl]
a. 똑같은, 동일한
▶ looking exactly alike, the same
▷ identify v. 구별하다, 확인하다
▷ identity n. 동일함, 신원

_____ _____

11 resemble [rizémbəl]
v. 닮다
▶ to look similar to another person or thing
▷ resemblance n. 유사

_____ _____

12 blessing [blésiŋ]
n. 축복
▶ a good thing, a happy circumstance
▷ bless v. 축복하다

_____ _____

13 pure-bred [pjuər bred]
a. (동물이) 순종인
▶ from the same bloodline or type, not mixed

_____ _____

14 cancer [kǽnsər]
n. 암
▶ a serious disease
▷ cancerous a. 암에 걸린

_____ _____

⑮ **intensive care unit**
[inténsiv kɛər júːnit]
중환자실(집중 치료실)
▶ a special hospital unit to treat patients in a critical situation

_____ _____

⑯ **heartbreaking** [háːtbrèikiŋ]
a. 마음이 아픈
▶ causing great pain

_____ _____

⑰ **mourn** [mɔːrn]
v. 슬퍼하다
▶ to be sad because someone has died
▶ mourning n. 슬픔
▶ mournful a. 슬픔에 잠긴

_____ _____

⑱ **funeral** [fjúːnərəl]
n. 장례식
▶ a ceremony after someone has died

_____ _____

⑲ **elegy** [élədʒi]
n. 애가
▶ a sad poem

_____ _____

⑳ **weep** [wiːp]
v. 울다
▶ to cry

_____ _____

㉑ **despair** [dispɛ́ər]
n. 절망 v. 절망감을 느끼다
▶ depression, hopelessness
▶ in despair 절망에 빠진

_____ _____

▶ 외우면서 단어를 2번씩 써보세요!

22 sympathize [símpəθàiz]
v. 공감하다, 동정하다
▶ to understand someone's feeling
▶ sympathy n. 공감, 동정
▶ sympathetic a. 공감하는, 동정하는

_____ _____

23 comfort [kÁmfərt]
v. 위로하다 n. 위로
▶ to make someone feel less worried or unhappy
▶ comfortable a. 편안한

_____ _____

24 unbearable [ʌ̀nbέərəbəl]
a. 견딜 수 없는
▶ unable to accept, intolerable
▶ bear v. 견디다
▶ bearable a. 견딜 수 있는

_____ _____

25 condolence [kəndóuləns]
n. 애도
▶ giving sympathy
▶ condole v. 위안하다, 문상하다

_____ _____

26 unanimously [juːnǽnəməsli]
ad. 만장일치로
▶ in a way everybody agrees, with one accord
▶ unanimity n. 만장일치
▶ unanimous a. 만장일치의

_____ _____

27 grave [greiv]
n. 무덤
▶ a place someone is buried in the ground after they die

_____ _____

28 immortal [imɔ́ːrtl]
a. 불멸의
▶ lasting forever and never dying, opposite of mortal
▶ immortality n. 영원함, 불멸

_____ _____

Exercise

A 주어진 뜻에 해당하는 단어를 보기에서 찾아 쓰세요.

| dye intensive care unit pregnant cancer resemble |
| balance pure-bred funeral companion heartbreaking |

① a person whom someone spends time with   _____
② to change one's hair color   _____
③ to be steady and not fall off   _____
④ having a baby inside one's body   _____
⑤ to look similar to another person or thing   _____
⑥ from the same bloodline or type, not mixed   _____
⑦ a serious disease   _____
⑧ a special hospital unit to treat patients in a critical situation   _____
⑨ causing great pain   _____
⑩ a ceremony after someone has died   _____

B 단어의 관계에 맞게 빈칸을 채우세요.

① _____ : bear = 견딜 수 없는 : 견디다
② _____ : grace = 상냥한 : 은혜
③ _____ : birth = 낳다 : 출생
④ adorable : adore = 귀여운 : _____
⑤ blessing : _____ = 축복 : 축복하다
⑥ cancer : _____ = 암 : 암에 걸린
⑦ identify : identity = 구별하다 : _____
⑧ resemble : resemblance = 닮다 : _____

C 의미가 같도록 알맞은 단어를 넣어 문장을 완성하세요.

1. Goodbye, Brownie. I'm sure you're in _____.
   잘 가, 브라우니. 나는 네가 천국에 있을 거라고 생각해.

2. You will stay _____ in our memories.
   너는 우리 기억 속에 영원히 남아 있을 거야

3. I read an _____.
   나는 애가를 읽었어.

4. You were _____.
   너는 운동 신경이 있었어.

5. I tried to _____ Sara.
   나는 사라를 위로하려고 했어.

6. They are all _____ like you.
   그들은 너처럼 모두 순종이야.

7. We _____ agreed to bury you.
   우리는 만장일치로 너를 묻어주기로 동의했어.

8. We put a_____stone above you with these words – Goodbye, Brownie.
   우리는 '잘 가, 브라우니'라는 말을 너의 묘비에 새겨 놓았어.

D 녹음된 내용을 듣고, 다음 빈칸에 들어갈 단어나 표현을 쓰세요.

Dear Brownie,

Goodbye, Brownie. I'm sure you're in _____. • Brownie, you were such a good _____ to Sara and me. • I remember how _____ you were. • We _____ your hair purple. • You were _____. • You could _____ on a board. • You liked tuna when you were _____. • Last month your three puppies were _____. • They are so _____. • Do you know the puppies are _____?

They _____ you. • Your puppies are a _____ to us. • They are all _____ like you. • We were shocked at the news that you had terminal _____. • Sara told me that you were taken to the _____ _____ _____. • I heard the _____ news. • This morning we all _____. • Sara said there would be a _____. • I read an _____. • Sara _____ all day. • She was in _____. • I _____ with her feelings.

I tried to _____ Sara. • It was _____ for her. • Other friends expressed their _____. • We _____ agreed to bury you. • We put a _____ stone above you with these words – Goodbye, Brownie. • You will stay _____ in our memories.

■ 녹음을 듣고, 해당하는 단어와 뜻을 쓰세요.

1	단어:	뜻:	2	단어:	뜻:
3	단어:	뜻:	4	단어:	뜻:
5	단어:	뜻:	6	단어:	뜻:
7	단어:	뜻:	8	단어:	뜻:
9	단어:	뜻:	10	단어:	뜻:
11	단어:	뜻:	12	단어:	뜻:
13	단어:	뜻:	14	단어:	뜻:
15	단어:	뜻:	16	단어:	뜻:
17	단어:	뜻:	18	단어:	뜻:
19	단어:	뜻:	20	단어:	뜻:
21	단어:	뜻:	22	단어:	뜻:
23	단어:	뜻:	24	단어:	뜻:
25	단어:	뜻:	26	단어:	뜻:
27	단어:	뜻:	28	단어:	뜻:
29	단어:	뜻:	30	단어:	뜻:

Voca Plus

접두사 in- / im-

접두사 in- / im- 은 단어 앞에 붙어 부정의 뜻을 만들어 주는 역할을 한다.
in-은 발음상의 편의를 위해 b, m, p 앞에 올 때 im-으로 변형된다.

in-

accurate 정확한
in + accurate = inaccurate 부정확한, 틀린
ex) It was an inaccurate quote of what I really said.
그것은 내가 실제로 했던 말을 정확하게 인용한 것이 아니었어요.

• ability 능력	inability 무능력
• definite 명확히 한정된	indefinite 한계가 없는
• gratitude 감사	ingratitude 배은망덕
• tolerable 참을 수 있는	intolerable 참을 수 없는
• credible 신뢰할 수 있는	incredible 믿을 수 없는
• hospitable 손님 접대를 잘하는	inhospitable 손님을 냉대하는
• voluntary 의도적인	involuntary 무의식 중의

im-

mortal 죽어야 할 운명의
im + mortal = immortal 불사의, 불멸의
ex) A human girl and an immortal vampire fall in love
인간인 소녀와 불사의 흡혈귀가 사랑에 빠져요.

• moral 도덕적인	immoral 부도덕한
• mobile 이동할 수 있는	immobile 움직일 수 없는
• practical 실용적인	impractical 비실용적인
• balance 균형	imbalance 불균형
• measurable 잴 수 있는	immeasurable 헤아릴 수 없는
• partial 편파적인	impartial 공명정대한
• purity 청결	impurity 불결

Culture Plus

Funeral 장례식

+ coffin 관 / + casket (고급스러운) 관

+ hearse 영구차

+ pallbearer 운구하는 사람, 관 곁에 따르는 사람

+ funeral home 장례식장

+ hold a wake 초상집에서의 밤샘을 치르다

+ express one's condolences to ~에게 조의를 표하다

+ give a eulogy 고인에 대한 송덕문을 낭독하다

SMART

Level.5

VOCA EDGE

Chapter 2

My home and Neighborhood

▶ 1단계 : 먼저 그림을 보고, 이 장의 에피소드를 추측해 보세요.

➔ **fight for dominance**

➔ **compliment someone**

Episode

Dear Daddy,

Daddy, do you agree that life is contradictory? ● Are you sure adults are mature? ● At times I assume kids are mature. ● Adults seem to miss their childhood. ● Like kids, at times they fight for dominance. ● Sometimes kids and adults need to reverse roles. ● You say your dictionary doesn't contain words such as fight.

You always say men are generous. ● Did I misunderstand you? ● Did you change your attitude? ● Last night my brother and I thought you and mommy put on an act. ● Both of you were absorbed in acting, but we could feel the cold atmosphere. ● We were aware that the situation was serious. ● Daddy, you looked troubled and concerned. ● You needed professional help. ● You seemed to be desperately looking for help. ● Ironically, that help came from me.

Hoony asked me, "Are they going to divorce?" ● I'm convinced that you can stop this from happening. ● Daddy, why don't you apologize first? ● Just admit to mom that she is right. ● Your generous act will impress her. ● Just compromise with her. ● Prove to her that you're not stubborn. ● Compliment her and tell her that she is the best wife and mother. ● Am I a good counselor for you?

1 contradictory [kàntrədíktəri]
a. 모순적인
- ▶ opposite to what someone expects or believes
- ▶ contradict v. 모순되다
- ▶ contradiction n. 모순

_____ _____

2 mature [mətʃúər]
a. 성숙한
- ▶ acting responsibly, fully grown, ripe
- ▶ maturity n. 성숙

_____ _____

3 assume [əsʃúːm]
v. 생각하다
- ▶ to think or believe something is true
- ▶ assumption n. 가정

_____ _____

4 childhood [tʃáildhùd]
n. 어린 시절
- ▶ the time period when someone is a child

_____ _____

5 dominance [dámənəns]
n. 우위, 주도권
- ▶ influence over other people
- ▶ dominate v. 우세하다, 지배하다
- ▶ dominant a. 우세한, 지배하는

_____ _____

6 reverse [rivə́ːrs]
v. 거꾸로 하다, 뒤집다
- ▶ to change positions with someone else
- ▶ reversal n. 역전, 반전

_____ _____

7 contain [kəntéin]
v. 포함하다
- ▶ to hold something inside
- ▶ container n. 용기

_____ _____

▶ 외우면서 단어를 2번씩 써보세요!

8 generous [dʒénərəs]
a. 관대한
▶ giving a lot, considerate
▶ generosity n. 관대

_____   _____

9 misunderstand
[mìsʌndərstǽnd]
v. 오해하다
▶ to make a mistake, not to understand
▶ misunderstanding n. 오해

_____   _____

10 attitude [ǽtitjùːd]
n. 사고방식, 태도
▶ a person's thoughts and feelings towards something

_____   _____

11 act [ækt]
n. 연기
▶ someone's behavior that does not express real feelings
▶ put on an act 연기하다

_____   _____

12 absorbed [əbsɔ́ːrbd]
a. 열중한
▶ very interested in something or someone
▶ absorption n. 열중
▶ be absorbed in ~에 열중하다, 몰두하다

_____   _____

13 atmosphere [ǽtməsfìər]
n. 분위기
▶ how a place or situation feels

_____   _____

14 situation [sìtʃuéiʃən]
n. 상황
▶ what is happening to someone at a specific time or period

_____   _____

어 · 휘 · 연 · 구

15 **concerned** [kənsə́:rnd]

a. 걱정하는

▶ worried or troubled about something
▶ concern v. 걱정하다 n. 걱정, 염려

_____ _____

16 **professional** [prəféʃənəl]

a. 전문적인 n. 전문가

▶ relating to a job which requires special training
▶ professionalism n. 전문성

_____ _____

17 **desperately** [déspəritli]

ad. 필사적으로

▶ badly, seriously
▶ desperation n. 자포자기
▶ desperate a. 필사적인

_____ _____

18 **ironically** [airánikəli]

ad. 아이러니하게도, 반어적으로

▶ unexpectedly, sarcastically
▶ irony n. 풍자

_____ _____

19 **divorce** [divɔ́:rs]

v. 이혼하다 n. 이혼

▶ to end a marriage
▶ divorced a. 이혼한

_____ _____

20 **convinced** [kənvínst]

a. 확신을 가진

▶ sure and certain, believing in something
▶ convince v. 확신시키다, 설득하다
▶ conviction n. 확신

_____ _____

21 **apologize** [əpálədʒàiz]

v. 사과하다

▶ to say sorry
▶ apology n. 사과

_____ _____

22 admit [ædmít]
v. 인정하다
▶ to tell the truth, to agree that something is true
▷ admission n. 승인

23 impress [imprés]
v. 감동시키다
▶ to make someone feel admired
▷ impression n. 감동, 인상
▷ impressive a. 인상적인

24 compromise [kámprəmàiz]
v. 화해하다 n. 화해
▶ to reach an agreement with someone

25 stubborn [stʌ́bərn]
a. 완고한
▶ unwilling to change one's mind
▷ stubbornness n. 완고
▷ stubbornly ad. 완고하게

26 compliment [kámpləmənt]
v. 칭찬하다 n. 칭찬
▶ to say something nice to someone, to praise
▷ complimentary a. 칭찬의, 무료의

27 counselor [káunsələr]
n. 상담자
▶ a person who gives advice
▷ counsel v. 상담하다 n. 상담
▷ counseling n. 카운셀링, 상담

Exercise

A 주어진 뜻에 해당하는 단어를 보기에서 찾아 쓰세요.

> contradictory   childhood   professional   misunderstand
> act   dominance   atmosphere   assume   situation attitude

① opposite to what someone expects or believes _____
② to think or believe something is true _____
③ the time period when someone is a child _____
④ influence over other people _____
⑤ to make a mistake, not to understand _____
⑥ a person's thoughts and feelings towards something _____
⑦ someone's behavior that does not express real feelings _____
⑧ how a place or situation feels _____
⑨ to what is happening to someone at a specific time or period _____
⑩ relating to a job which requires special training _____

B 단어의 관계에 맞게 빈칸을 채우세요.

① counselor : counsel = _____ : 상담하다
② impress : impressive = 감동시키다 : _____
③ _____ : admission = 인정하다 : 승인
④ ironically : irony = 반어적으로 : _____
⑤ contain : _____ = 포함하다 : 용기
⑥ dominance : _____ = 우위 : 우세하다
⑦ reverse : reversal = 뒤집다 : _____
⑧ mature : _____ = 성숙한 : 성숙

C 의미가 같도록 알맞은 단어를 넣어 문장을 완성하세요.

1. _____ her and tell her that she is the best wife and mother.
   그녀를 칭찬하고 그녀가 최고의 아내이자 엄마라고 말하세요.

2. Prove to her that you're not _____.
   완고하지 않다는 걸 그녀에게 증명해 보이세요.

3. Just _____ with her.
   그냥 그녀와 화해하세요.

4. Daddy, why don't you _____ first?
   아빠, 아빠가 먼저 사과하시는 게 어때요?

5. I'm _____ that you can stop this from happening.
   저는 아빠가 이런 일을 막을 수 있다고 확신해요.

6. Hoony asked me, "Are they going to _____?"
   후니는 저에게 "두 분이 이혼하실까?"라고 물었어요.

7. You seemed to be _____ looking for help.
   필사적으로 도움을 찾고 있는 것 같았어요.

8. You needed _____ help.
   전문적인 도움이 필요했어요.

D 녹음된 내용을 듣고, 다음 빈칸에 들어갈 단어나 표현을 쓰세요.

Dear Daddy,

Daddy, do you agree that life is _____? ● Are you sure adults are _____? ● At times I _____ kids are mature. ● Adults seem to miss their _____. ● Like kids, at times they fight for _____. ● Sometimes kids and adults need to _____ roles. ● You you're your dictionary doesn't _____ words such as fight.

You always say men are _____. ● Did I _____ you? ● Did you change your _____? ● Last night my brother and I thought you and mommy put on an _____. ● Both of you were _____ in acting, but we could feel the cold _____. ● We were aware that the _____ was serious. ● Daddy, you looked troubled and _____. ● You needed _____ help. ● You seemed to be _____ looking for help. ● _____, that help came from me.

Hoony asked me, "Are they going to _____?" ● I'm _____ that you can stop this from happening. ● Daddy, why don't you _____ first? ● Just admit to mom that she is right. ● Your generous act will _____ her. ● Just _____ with her. ● Prove to her that you're not _____. ● _____ her and tell her that she is the best wife and mother. ● Am I a good _____ for you?

Chapter 2
My home and Neighborhood

▶ 1단계 : 먼저 그림을 보고, 이 장의 에피소드를 추측해 보세요.

→ quarantine something from someone ●

● begin to ascend ←

→ embrace something ●

Episode

Today is a sad and happy day. ● Sara's family emigrated to the U.S. and I got an email from her.

Dear Bomi,

Bomi, it is so complicated to leave for another country. ● Yesterday my pet, Choko, was vaccinated. ● Choko had an immunization shot. ● This morning my family went to the international airport. ● It's much bigger than the domestic airport.

First, we checked our baggage. ● Then, we went through the next procedure. ● An officer tried to quarantine Choko from me. ● Please don't separate us. ● I pleaded with him. ● But my pleas were in vain. ● He carried Choko to a freight cabin. ● I wondered when we would reunite. ● I asked if I could go with Choko, but he said it was a restricted area. ● I went through security. ● What's that metal detector for? ● I saw that it inspected everything. ● I boarded the plane.

The captain announced that we must fasten our seat belts. ● The plane began to ascend. ● On the ground, houses started to shrink. ● Can you imagine flying at an altitude of 42,000 feet? ● Suddenly, the plane started shaking and I felt threatened. ● Finally, the plane landed and I embraced Choko. ● After the 18 hour flight, I experienced jet lag and I was extremely tired. ● It was a really hard day.

어·휘·연·구

▶ 3단계 : 외우면서 단어를 2번씩 써보세요!

1 **emigrate** [éməgrèit]

v. 이민가다

▶ to leave one's home country to live in another country
▶ emigration n. 이주

_____ _____

2 **complicated** [kámpləkèitid]

a. 복잡한

▶ difficult and complex, opposite of simple
▶ complicate v. 복잡하게 하다
▶ complication n. 복잡

_____ _____

3 **vaccinate** [vǽksənèit]

v. 예방접종을 하다

▶ to give medicine to prevent disease
▶ vaccination n. 예방접종

_____ _____

4 **immunization** [ìmjunizéiʃən]

n. 예방 주사

▶ medicine that prevents a disease from affecting someone
▶ immunize v. 면역시키다
▶ immune a. 면역의

_____ _____

5 **international** [ìntərnǽʃənəl]

a. 국제적인

▶ involving many countries

_____ _____

6 **domestic** [douméstik]

a. 국내의

▶ involving only one's own country
▶ domesticate v. 길들이다

_____ _____

7 **baggage** [bǽgidʒ]

n. 짐

▶ travelling bags, luggage

_____ _____

▶ 외우면서 단어를 2번씩 써보세요!

8 **procedure** [prəsíːdʒər]
n. 절차
▶ a process, a way of doing something

_____ _____

9 **quarantine** [kwɔ́ːrəntìːn]
v. 격리시키다, 검역하다
n. 격리, 검역
▶ to separate or remove one thing from another

_____ _____

10 **separate** [sépərèit]
v. 떼어놓다, 분리하다
▶ to pull two things apart so they are not joined
▶ separation n. 분리

_____ _____

11 **plead** [pliːd]
v. 간청하다

to beg, to ask with strong feelings
▶ plea n. 탄원
▶ plead with ~에게 간청하다

_____ _____

12 **vain** [vein]
n. 허사
▶ failure in achieving what was intended
▶ in vain 허사인, 쓸모없는

_____ _____

13 **freight** [freit]
n. 화물
▶ goods that are transported separately from personal items

_____ _____

14 **reunite** [rìːjuːnáit]
v. 재회하다
▶ to see someone again after having been separated
▶ reunification n. 재회, 통일

_____ _____

15 restricted [ristríktid]

a. 제한된

▶ allowed to only people with special permission; limited
▶ restrict v. 제한하다
▶ restriction n. 제한

_____   _____

16 security [sikjúəriti]

n. 보안

▶ all the measures taken to protect a place
▶ secure v. 확보하다 a. 안전한

_____   _____

17 detector [ditéktər]

n. 탐지기

▶ a machine used to look for items in people's luggage
▶ detect v. 탐지하다
▶ detection n. 탐지

_____   _____

18 inspect [inspékt]

v. 검사하다

▶ to carefully look at something to check if it is okay
▶ inspection n. 검사

_____   _____

19 board [bɔːrd]

v. 탑승하다

▶ to get into the plane

_____   _____

20 fasten [fǽsn]

v. 묶다

▶ to close something

_____   _____

▶ 외우면서 단어를 2번씩 써보세요!

㉑ ascend [əsénd]
v. 올라가다
▶ to move upwards
▶ ascension n. 상승

_____   _____

㉒ shrink [ʃriŋk]
v. 작아지다
▶ to become smaller in size

_____   _____

㉓ altitude [ǽltətʃùːd]
n. 고도
▶ the height above sea level

_____   _____

㉔ threatened [θrétnd]
a. 무서운
▶ worried, feared or bullied
▶ threaten v. 협박하다
▶ threat n. 협박

_____   _____

㉕ embrace [embréis]
v. 껴안다
▶ to hug

_____   _____

㉖ jet lag [dʒet læg]
시차로 인한 피로
▶ a feeling of tiredness after a long flight

_____   _____

㉗ extremely [ikstríːmli]
ad. 매우
▶ more than expected, very much (superlative)
▶ extreme n. 극단 a. 극심한

_____   _____

Exercise

A 주어진 뜻에 해당하는 단어를 보기에서 찾아 쓰세요.

> domestic   vaccinate   international   baggage   quarantine
> immunization   complicated   procedure   freight   emigrate

① to leave one's home country to live in another country _____
② difficult and complex, opposite of simple _____
③ to give medicine to prevent disease _____
④ medicine that prevents a disease from affecting someone _____
⑤ involving many countries _____
⑥ involving only one's own country _____
⑦ travelling bags, luggage _____
⑧ to a process, a way of doing something _____
⑨ to separate or remove one thing from another _____
⑩ goods that are transported separately from personal items _____

B 단어의 관계에 맞게 빈칸을 채우세요.

① plead : _____ = 간청하다 : 탄원
② vain : _____ = 허사 : 허사인
③ security : secure = 보안 : _____
④ _____ : detect = 탐지기 : 탐지하다
⑤ inspect : _____ = 검사하다 : 검사
⑥ ascend : ascension = 올라가다 : 상승
⑦ _____ : extreme = 매우 : 극단
⑧ domestic : domesticate = 국내의 : _____

C 의미가 같도록 알맞은 단어를 넣어 문장을 완성하세요.

1. After the 18 hour flight, I experienced jet lag and I was _____ tired.
   18시간의 비행 후에 나는 시차로 인한 피로를 느꼈고 매우 지쳐 있었어.

2. Finally, the plane landed and I _____ Choko.
   마침내 비행기는 착륙했고 나는 초코를 꺼안아 주었어

3. Suddenly, the plane started shaking and I felt _____.
   갑자기 비행기가 흔들리기 시작했고 나는 무서웠어.

4. Can you imagine flying at an _____ of 42,000 feet?
   42,000피트의 고도에서 날아가는 걸 상상할 수 있니?

5. On the ground, houses started to _____.
   땅에 있는 집들이 작아지기 시작했어.

6. The captain announced that we must _____ our seat belts.
   기장은 우리가 안전벨트를 매야 한다고 방송했어.

7. I _____ the plane.
   나는 비행기에 올랐어.

8. I asked if I could go with Choko, but he said it was a _____ area.
   나는 초코와 함께 갈 수 있는지 물어보았지만, 그는 그곳이 제한 구역이라고 말했어.

D 녹음된 내용을 듣고, 다음 빈칸에 들어갈 단어나 표현을 쓰세요.

Today is a sad and happy day. ● Sara's family _____ to the U.S. and I got an email from her.

Dear Bomi,

Bomi, it is so _____ to leave for another country. ● Yesterday my pet, Choko, was _____. ● Choko had an _____ shot. ● This morning my family went to the _____ airport. ● It's much bigger than the _____ airport.

First, we checked our _____. ● Then, we went through the next _____. ● An officer tried to _____ Choko from me. ● Please don't _____ us. ● I _____ with him. ● But my pleas were in _____. ● He carried Choko to a _____ cabin. ● I wondered when we would _____. ● I asked if I could go with Choko, but he said it was a _____ area. ● I went through _____. ● What's that metal _____ for? ● I saw that it _____ everything. ● I _____ the plane.

The captain announced that we must _____ our seat belts. ● The plane began to _____. ● On the ground, houses started to _____. ● Can you imagine flying at an _____ of 42,000 feet? ● Suddenly, the plane started shaking and I felt _____. ● Finally, the plane landed and I _____ Choko. ● After the 18 hour flight, I experienced ___ ____ and I was _____ tired. ● It was a really hard day.●

My home and Neighborhood

▶ 1단계 : 먼저 그림을 보고, 이 장의 에피소드를 추측해 보세요.

→ **consist of 5 oceans and 6 continents** ●

● **see polar bears inhabiting the ice** ←

→ **go to Antarctica and see emperor penguins** ●

Episode

Dear Sara,

Sara, I'm looking at the globe. ● I enclosed a map in your envelope. ● Today I had a geography class. ● I learned that the earth consists of 5 oceans and 6 continents. ● Sara, can you find your continent? ● It's just a few inches away from Korea, right? ● How did people discover that earth is oval, not square?

Can you see the equator line in the center? ● It's lucky that we are not living in a tropical area. ● I remember how much we hate hot and humid weather. ● Imagine living in weather that is 40 degrees Celsius. ● It's equivalent to 104 degrees Fahrenheit. ● Isn't it lucky that we live in mild climates? ● Luckily, we live in a temperate zone. ● We both live in the northern hemisphere. ● In the southern hemisphere, it must be summer now. ● See the horizontal lines? ● I mean the parallel lines.

If you move your finger north, you can find the Arctic ocean. ● Someday we'll go on a cruise tour together to see the glaciers. ● We can see vast glaciers there. ● We will see polar bears inhabiting the ice. ● Or we can go to Antarctica and see emperor penguins. ● Do you know what is related to the time difference? ● You can see vertical lines. ● They are called longitude lines. ● Sara, I wonder what the population of your city is. ● What kind of plants do people cultivate there?

▶ 3단계 : 외우면서 단어를 2번씩 써보세요!

1 **globe** [gloub]
n. 지구본
▶ a model of the earth
▶ global a. 세계적인

_____ _____

2 **enclose** [enklóuz]
v. 동봉하다
▶ to put something inside an envelope

_____ _____

3 **geography** [dʒi:ágrəfi]
n. 지리학
▶ the study of the countries of the world
▶ geographical a. 지리학적인

_____ _____

4 **consist** [kənsíst]
v. 이루어져 있다
▶ to be made of separate things
▶ consist of ~로 이루어져 있다

_____ _____

5 **continent** [kántənənt]
n. 대륙
▶ a large area of land that consists of several countries
▶ continental a. 대륙의

_____ _____

6 **inch** [intʃ]
n. 인치
▶ a unit for measuring distances

_____ _____

7 **oval** [óuvəl]
a. 타원형의
▶ shaped like a circle but slightly flat and longer

_____ _____

8 **equator** [ikwéitər]
n. 적도
▶ a line around the center of the earth

_____ _____

▶ 외우면서 단어를 2번씩 써보세요!

⑨ tropical [trápikəl]
a. 열대의
▶ referring to the hottest part of the earth
▶ tropics n. 열대 지방

_____ _____

⑩ humid [hjúːmid]
a. 후덥지근한, 습한
▶ referring to weather that is hot and very damp
▶ humidity n. 습기

_____ _____

⑪ Celsius [sélsiəs]
n. 섭씨
▶ a unit for measuring temperature

_____ _____

⑫ equivalent [ikwívələnt]
a. 동등한 n. 동등물
▶ the same, alike, being equal
▶ equivalence n. 동등함
▶ equivalent to ~에 상당하는

_____ _____

⑬ mild [maild]
a. 온화한
▶ relating to weather that is not very hot or very cold

_____ _____

⑭ temperate [témpərit]
a. 온대의, 성품 등이 온화한
▶ neither extremely hot nor too cold, mild

_____ _____

⑮ zone [zoun]
n. 지역, 지대
▶ an area that has particular features

_____ _____

16 **hemisphere** [hémisfiər]
n. 반구
▶ one half of the earth

_____   _____

17 **southern** [sʌ́ðərn]
a. 남쪽의
▶ in the south side, opposite of northern

_____   _____

18 **horizontal** [hɔ̀ːrəzántl]
a. 수평의, 가로의
▶ sideways, opposite of vertical
▶ horizon n. 지평선
▶ horizontally ad. 수평으로

_____   _____

19 **parallel** [pǽrəlèl]
a. 평행한
▶ being the same distance along the whole length

_____   _____

20 **Arctic** [áːrktik]
n. 북극 a. 북극의
▶ the very cold area around the North Pole

_____   _____

21 **glacier** [gléiʃər]
n. 빙하
▶ a large mass of ice on land
▶ glacial a. 빙하의

_____   _____

22 **vast** [væst]
a. 거대한
▶ big, huge, very large and wide
▶ vastly ad. 광대하게

_____   _____

▶ 외우면서 단어를 2번씩 써보세요!

㉓ inhabit [inhǽbit]
v. 살다
▶ to live in a place
▶ inhabitant n. 거주자
▶ inhabitation n. 거주

_____   _____

㉔ Antarctica [æntáːrktikə]
n. 남극
▶ the very large cold area around the South Pole

_____   _____

㉕ related [riléitid]
a. 관련이 있는
▶ connected, associated
▶ relate v. 관련시키다
▶ relation n. 관계

_____   _____

㉖ vertical [vɔ́ːrtikəl]
a. 수직의, 세로의
▶ going upwards, going from top to bottom
▶ vertically ad. 수직으로

_____   _____

㉗ longitude [lάndʒətjùːd]
n. 경도
▶ imaginary lines around the earth that show the position of things

_____   _____

㉘ population [pὰpjəléiʃən]
n. 인구
▶ all the people or things that live in a place
▶ populate v. 거주시키다
▶ populated a. 거주하는

_____   _____

㉙ cultivate [kʌ́ltəvèit]
v. 경작하다
▶ to grow or develop
▶ cultivation n. 경작

_____   _____

Exercise

A 주어진 뜻에 해당하는 단어를 보기에서 찾아 쓰세요.

population	equivalent	Antarctica	oval	mild
horizontal	parallel	temperate	Arctic	longitude

① all the people or things that live in a place _____
② imaginary lines around the earth that show the position of things _____
③ the very large cold area around the South Pole _____
④ the very cold area around the North Pole _____
⑤ being the same distance along the whole length _____
⑥ sideways, opposite of vertical _____
⑦ the same, alike, being equal _____
⑧ relating to weather that is not very hot or very cold _____
⑨ neither extremely hot nor too cold, mild _____
⑩ shaped like a circle but slightly flat and longer _____

B 단어의 관계에 맞게 빈칸을 채우세요.

① globe : global = 지구본 : _____
② tropical : tropics = 열대의 : _____
③ _____ : humidity = 습한 : 습기
④ _____ : glacial = 빙하 : 빙하의
⑤ vast : _____ = 거대한 : 광대하게
⑥ relate : _____ = 관련시키다 : 관련이 있는
⑦ consist : _____ = 이루어져있다 : ~로 이루어져있다
⑧ horizon : horizontally = 지평선 : _____

C 의미가 같도록 알맞은 단어를 넣어 문장을 완성하세요.

1. What kind of plants do people _____ there?
   거기에서는 사람들이 어떤 식물을 경작하니?

2. They are called _____ lines.
   그 선들은 경선이라고 불려.

3. You can see _____ lines.
   수직으로 된 선이 보일 거야.

4. We will see polar bears _____ the ice.
   우리는 얼음에서 사는 북극곰을 볼 거야.

5. I mean the _____ lines.
   평행한 선 말이야.

6. In the _____ hemisphere, it must be summer now.
   남반구는 지금 여름일 거야.

7. We both live in the northern _____.
   우리는 둘 다 북반구에 살아.

8. Luckily, we live in a temperate _____.
   다행히도, 우리는 온대 지역에 살고 있어.

D 녹음된 내용을 듣고, 다음 빈칸에 들어갈 단어나 표현을 쓰세요.

Dear Sara,

Sara, I'm looking at the _____. ● I _____ a map in your envelope. ●Today I had a _____ class. ● I learned that the earth _____ of 5 oceans and 6 continents. ● Sara, can you find your _____? ● It's just a few inches away from Korea, right? ● How did people discover that earth is _____, not square?

Can you see the _____ line in the center? ● It's lucky that we are not living in a _____ area. ● I remember how much we hate hot and _____ weather. ● Imagine living in weather that is 40 degrees _____. ● It's _____ to 104 degrees Fahrenheit. ● Isn't it lucky that we live in _____ climates? ● Luckily, we live in a _____ _____. ● We both live in the northern _____. ● In the _____ hemisphere, it must be summer now. ● See the _____ lines? ● I mean the _____ lines.

If you move your finger north, you can find the _____ ocean. ● Someday we'll go on a cruise tour together to see the _____. ● We can see _____ glaciers there. ● We will see polar bears _____ the ice. ● Or we can go to _____ and see emperor penguins. ● Do you know what is _____ to the time difference? ● You can see _____ lines. ● They are called _____ lines. ● Sara, I wonder what the _____ of your city is. ● What kind of plants do people _____ there? ●

■ 녹음을 듣고, 해당하는 단어와 뜻을 쓰세요.

1	단어:	뜻:	2	단어:	뜻:
3	단어:	뜻:	4	단어:	뜻:
5	단어:	뜻:	6	단어:	뜻:
7	단어:	뜻:	8	단어:	뜻:
9	단어:	뜻:	10	단어:	뜻:
11	단어:	뜻:	12	단어:	뜻:
13	단어:	뜻:	14	단어:	뜻:
15	단어:	뜻:	16	단어:	뜻:
17	단어:	뜻:	18	단어:	뜻:
19	단어:	뜻:	20	단어:	뜻:
21	단어:	뜻:	22	단어:	뜻:
23	단어:	뜻:	24	단어:	뜻:
25	단어:	뜻:	26	단어:	뜻:
27	단어:	뜻:	28	단어:	뜻:
29	단어:	뜻:	30	단어:	뜻:

Voca Plus

접두사 re- / en-

re-는 'again,' 'back'이라는 뜻의 접두사로, '무언가를 반복하거나 되돌려놓다'라는 뜻의 단어를 만든다. en-은 'make'라는 뜻의 접두사로, '어떤 상태가 되게 하다'라는 뜻의 단어를 만든다.

re-

assign 임명하다
re + assign = reassign 재임명하다
ex) I've been reassigned to another department.
나는 다른 부서로 재임명되었어요.

• act 행하다	react 반응하다
• bound 튀어오르다	rebound 다시 튀어오르다
• fresh 새로워지다	refresh 원기를 회복하다
• formation 형성	reformation 개조
• habilitate 훈련시키다	rehabilitate 사회 복귀시키다
• imburse 지불하다	reimburse 상환하다
• consider 고려하다	reconsider 재고하다

en-

large 큰
en + large = enlarge 크게 하다
ex) How big should we enlarge these photos?
이 사진들을 얼마나 크게 확대시킬까요?

• courage 용기	encourage 용기를 북돋우다
• compass 한계, 범위	encompass 둘러싸다, 포위하다
• title 직위, 권리	entitle 칭호를 주다, 권리를 주다
• tail 꼬리, 끝	entail 수반하다
• trap 덫	entrap 덫에 걸리게 하다, 함정에 빠뜨리다
• vision 상상력, 미래상	envision 상상하다, 계획하다
• twine 꼰 실	entwine 얽히게 하다

Culture Plus

Climate 기후

+ temperate zone 온대

+ subtropical zone 아열대

+ tropical zone 열대

+ subpolar zone 냉대

+ polar zone 한대

+ oceanic climate 해양성 기후

+ continental climate 대륙성 기후

Chapter 3 Learning

▶ 1단계 : 먼저 그림을 보고, 이 장의 에피소드를 추측해 보세요.

→ **live together with dinosaurs**

speculate and observe things ←

→ **make hypotheses and theories**

Dear Sara,

Our class went to a natural science museum. ● One of the most interesting things was that it was powered by renewable energy. ● We were surprised to learn that the huge buildings were heated by solar energy. ● We went upstairs and looked at the exhibits on display. ● They included remains from our ancestors. ● We also saw fossils. ● Our teacher explained that some organisms became fossilized. ● They can show us how life originated. ● There were even dinosaur bones. ● They were enormous. ● Sara, isn't it a relief that we don't live together with dinosaurs? ● We saw dinosaur skulls, too. ● The displays showed how humans evolved. ● Anthropologists believe that humans evolved from apes. ● Sara, can you imagine our great, great ancestors were apes?

We moved over to the astronomy section. ● The displays there explained how our universe originated from a dot. ● The dot exploded. ● Then it expanded. ● Wow, our universe is full of mystery. ● How can scientists analyze such a vast universe? ● It must have given them chronic headaches. ● Maybe they took painkillers to help them think. ● I thought for a few moments about the ancient Greek philosophers. ● How were they able to explain natural phenomena? ● Our teacher said they speculated a lot. ● They observed things and made hypotheses. ● They also made many theories. ● Whew, what a complicated process!

어·휘·연·구

▶ 3단계 : 외우면서 단어를 2번씩 써보세요!

1 renewable [rinjúːwəbəl]
a. 재생 가능한
▶ constantly replenishing
▶ renew v. 새롭게 하다
▶ renewable energy 재생 에너지

_____ _____

2 heat [hiːt]
v. 난방을 하다, 가열하다
▶ to raise the temperature inside the buildings

_____ _____

3 solar [sóulər]
a. 태양의
▶ relating to the sun

_____ _____

4 exhibit [igzíbit]
n. 전시품 v. 전시하다
▶ a thing that is displayed for people to look at
▶ exhibition n. 전시

_____ _____

5 remains [riméinz]
n. 유해
▶ the parts of a living thing's body that remain after it dies
▶ remain v. 잔존하다
▶ remainder n. 나머지

_____ _____

6 fossil [fásl]
n. 화석
▶ the hardened body of an old animal or plant
▶ fossilize v. 화석으로 만들다

_____ _____

7 organism [ɔ́ːrgənìzəm]
n. 생물
▶ any plant or animal, anything that is alive

_____ _____

▶ 외우면서 단어를 2번씩 써보세요!

8 **originate** [ərídʒənèit]
v. 생기다, 유래하다
▶ to come into existence, to start
▷ origin n. 기원
▷ origination n. 시작, 발생

_____   _____

9 **bone** [boun]
n. 뼈
▶ the hard parts inside one's body that make one's skeleton
▷ bony a. 뼈만 남은, 앙상한

_____   _____

10 **enormous** [inɔ́ːrməs]
a. 거대한
▶ very large, huge

_____   _____

11 **relief** [rilíːf]
n. 안심
▶ a feeling of gladness that something bad did not happen
▷ relieve v. 경감시키다

_____   _____

12 **skull** [skʌl]
n. 해골
▷ the bones of a head

_____   _____

13 **evolve** [iválv]
v. 진화하다
▶ to change gradually over a long time into a better form
▷ evolution n. 진화, 발전
▷ evolutionary a. 진화의

_____   _____

14 **anthropologist**
[ænθrəpá, lədʒist]
n. 인류학자
▶ a scientist who studies people, society, and culture
▷ anthropology n. 인류학

_____   _____

▶ 3단계 : 외우면서 단어를 2번씩 써보세요!

15 ape [eip]
n. 유인원
▶ an animal that is similar to a monkey

_____   _____

16 section [sékʃən]
n. 구역, 부분
▶ division, one of the parts of something

_____   _____

17 universe [júːnəvə̀ːrs]
n. 우주
▶ the earth, stars, and planets
▷ universal a. 전 세계적인, 보편적인

_____   _____

18 explode [iksplóud]
v. 폭발하다
▶ to loudly burst and break apart
▷ explosion n. 폭발

_____   _____

19 expand [ikspǽnd]
v. 팽창하다
▶ to become larger
▷ expansion n. 팽창

_____   _____

20 mystery [místəri]
n. 신비
▶ something that is strange and can't be explained

_____   _____

21 analyze [ǽnəlàiz]
v. 분석하다
▶ to think about something in order to understand it
▷ analysis n. 분석

_____   _____

22 chronic [kránik]
a. 만성의
▶ very painful and lasting a long time

_____   _____

▶ 외우면서 단어를 2번씩 써보세요!

23 painkiller [péinkìlər]
n. 진통제
▶ medicine that makes pain go away

_____ _____

24 philosopher [filásəfər]
n. 철학자
▶ a person who studies and creates ideas about many things
▶ philosophy n. 철학

_____ _____

25 phenomenon [finámənàn]
n. 현상
▶ an event, a thing that happens
▶ phenomena (phenomenon의 복수형)

_____ _____

26 speculate [spékjəlèit]
v. 사색하다, 깊이 생각하다
▶ to think about something, to wonder

_____ _____

27 observe [əbzə́:rv]
v. 관찰하다
▶ to examine something, to discern
▶ observant a. 관찰하는

_____ _____

28 hypothesis [haipáθəsis]
n. 가설
▶ an idea that attempts to explain how something happens
▶ hypothesize v. 가설을 세우다
▶ hypothetical a. 가설의

_____ _____

29 theory [θíəri]
n. 이론
▶ an idea that is intended to explain something
▶ theorize v. 이론을 세우다
▶ theoretical a. 이론의

_____ _____

Exercise

A 주어진 뜻에 해당하는 단어를 보기에서 찾아 쓰세요.

> heat   skull   chronic   painkiller   solar
> section   anthropologist   ape   philosopher   organism

① to raise the temperature inside the buildings _____
② relating to the sun _____
③ any plant or animal, anything that is alive _____
④ the bones of a head _____
⑤ a scientist who studies people, society, and culture _____
⑥ an animal that is similar to a monkey or a gorilla _____
⑦ division, one of the parts of something _____
⑧ very painful and lasting a long time _____
⑨ medicine that makes pain go away _____
⑩ a person who studies and creates ideas about many things _____

B 단어의 관계에 맞게 빈칸을 채우세요.

① theory : _____ = 이론 : 이론을 세우다
② analyze : _____ = 분석하다 : 분석
③ expand : _____ = 팽창하다 : 팽창
④ _____ : explosion = 팽창하다 : 팽창
⑤ universe : universal = 우주 : _____
⑥ bone : _____ = 뼈 : 뼈만 남은
⑦ originate : _____ = 생기다 : 기원
⑧ remains : remain = 유해 : _____

C 의미가 같도록 알맞은 단어를 넣어 문장을 완성하세요.

1. They observed things and made _____.
   그들은 사물을 관찰했고 가설을 만들었어.

2. One of the most interesting things was that it was powered by_____energy.
   가장 흥미 있는 것 중 하나는 재생 에너지를 연료로 쓴다는 사실이었어.

3. Our teacher said they _____ a lot.
   우리 선생님은 그들이 많은 사색을 했다고 말씀하셨어.

4. How were they able to explain natural _____?
   그들은 어떻게 자연 현상을 설명할 수 있었을까?

5. I thought for a few moments about the ancient Greek _____.
   나는 잠시 동안 고대 그리스 철학자들에 대해 생각해 보았어.

6. Wow, our universe is full of _____.
   와, 우리의 우주는 신비로 가득 차 있어.

7. Sara, can you imagine our great, great ancestors were _____?
   사라, 우리의 아주 먼 조상이 유인원이었다는 걸 상상할 수 있니?

8. _____ believe that humans evolved from apes.
   인류학자들은 인간이 유인원에서 진화되었다고 믿고 있어

D 녹음된 내용을 듣고, 다음 빈칸에 들어갈 단어나 표현을 쓰세요. 🎧

Dear Sara,

Our class went to a natural science museum. ◦ One of the most interesting things was that it was powered by _____ energy. ◦ We were surprised to learn that the huge buildings were _____ by _____ energy. ◦ We went upstairs and looked at the _____ on display. ◦ They included _____ from our ancestors. ◦ We also saw _____. ◦ Our teacher explained that some _____ became fossilized. ◦ They can show us how life _____. ◦ There were even dinosaur _____. ◦ They were _____. ◦ Sara, isn't it a _____ that we don't live together with dinosaurs? ◦ We saw dinosaur _____, too. ◦ The displays showed how humans _____. ◦ _____ believe that humans evolved from apes. ◦ Sara, can you imagine our great, great ancestors were _____?

We moved over to the astronomy _____. ◦ The displays there explained how our _____ originated from a dot. ◦ The dot _____. ◦ Then it _____. ◦ Wow, our universe is full of _____. ◦ How can scientists _____ such a vast universe? ◦ It must have given them _____ headaches. ◦ Maybe they took _____ to help them think. ◦ I thought for a few moments about the ancient Greek _____. ◦ How were they able to explain natural phenomena? ◦ Our teacher said they _____ a lot. ◦ They _____ things and made _____. ◦ They also made many _____. ◦ Whew, what a complicated process!

▶ 1단계 : 먼저 그림을 보고, 이 장의 에피소드를 추측해 보세요.

→ **assemble in the auditorium**

→ **look up and serenade someone**

Dear Diary,

My uncle is a college student. ● He gained admission to a prestigious college. ● It has the best reputation in Korea. ● After the entrance ceremony, there was an orientation for freshmen. ● Students and guests assembled in the auditorium. ● It was big enough to accommodate about 5,000 people. ● The principal praised the students. ● He said how competent they were.

Then he introduced the faculty members. ● After that, he explained the guidelines of campus life. ● Then the school advisor came on stage. ● She said being a college student is a big responsibility. ● She explained how they assess students and she talked about how important term papers are. ● Whew, three years of cramming and studying? ● How do students tolerate it? ● Don't they deserve time off to play? ● After the ceremony, we went to the dormitory where my uncle will stay. ● It didn't look very luxurious. ● There was a laundromat on the first floor. ● Students can do laundry there. ● There were signs on the doors of some rooms that said "Do not make disturbances." ● Although the school was co-ed, the girls' dormitory was separate. ● It reminded me of the play, Romeo and Juliet. ● Romeo looked up at Juliet's window and serenaded her. ● My uncle seemed to be disappointed that the dormitories were separate. ● There are supervisors in the girls' dormitory. ● They rotate their shifts every night. ● Don't be disappointed, uncle. ● You can climb a ladder to the girls' dormitory if you find a perfect match.

1 **college** [kálidʒ]
n. 대학교
▶ a place where students study to get a qualification like a university

_____ _____

2 **prestigious** [prestídʒiəs]
a. 일류의, 명문의
▶ well-known, important and admired
▶ prestige n. 명성, 평판

_____ _____

3 **reputation** [rèpjətéiʃən]
n. 명성, 평판
▶ people's opinion about how good something is
▶ reputable a. 평판이 좋은

_____ _____

4 **orientation** [ɔ̀:rientéiʃən]
n. 오리엔테이션
▶ an event where students receive helpful information about the college
▶ orientate v. 환경에 순응하다, 적응시키다

_____ _____

5 **assemble** [əsémbəl]
v. 모이다
▶ to come together
▶ assembly n. 집회

_____ _____

6 **accommodate** [əkámədèit]
v. 수용하다
▶ to provide for, to supply with food, housing, etc.
▶ accommodation n. 수용

_____ _____

7 **praise** [preiz]
v. 칭찬하다 n. 칭찬
▶ to compliment and say nice things about something
▶ praiseworthy a. 칭찬할 만한

_____ _____

▶ 외우면서 단어를 2번씩 써보세요!

8 competent [kámpətənt]
a. 유능한
▶ having ability, talents, and skills
▷ competence n. 능력

_____ _____

9 faculty [fǽkəlti]
n. 교직원
▶ the staff of a college or university

_____ _____

10 guideline [gáidlàin]
n. 지침
▶ a set of rules and instructions that tell someone how to behave

_____ _____

11 advisor [ædváizər]
n. 신입생 지도 교수
▶ a person who gives advice
▷ advise v. 충고하다
▷ advice n. 충고

_____ _____

12 responsibility [rispʌ̀nsəbíləti]
n. 책임
▶ a duty that someone has because of their job or position
▷ responsible a. 책임이 있는

_____ _____

13 assess [əsés]
v. 평가하다
▶ to test, to evaluate
▷ assessment n. 평가, 감정

_____ _____

14 term paper [tə:rm péipər]
학기말 리포트
▶ a long document that students must write and which they will receive a grade for

_____ _____

15 tolerate [tálərèit]
v. 견디다
▶ to cope or deal with a situation
▶ tolerance n. 관용 ▶ toleration n. 묵인
▶ tolerant a. 관대한 ▶ tolerable a. 참을 수 있는

_____ _____

16 deserve [dizə́:rv]
v. ~할 만하다, ~할 자격이 있다
▶ to have a legitimate claim to have or receive something
▶ deserving a. ~할 가치 있는

_____ _____

17 dormitory [dɔ́:rmətɔ̀:ri]
n. 기숙사
▶ a place where students live on campus

_____ _____

18 luxurious [lʌgʒúəriəs]
a. 호화스러운
▶ comfortable and expensive
▶ luxury n. 사치

_____ _____

19 laundromat [lɔ́:ndrəmæt]
n. 빨래방
▶ a room with machines where someone can wash their clothes

_____ _____

20 laundry [lɔ́:ndri]
n. 세탁물, 빨래
▶ dirty clothes that need to be washed
▶ do laundry 세탁하다

_____ _____

21 disturbance [distə́:rbəns]
n. 방해, 소란
▶ disturbing something, bother, acts that annoy or irritate people
▶ disturb v. 방해하다
▶ disturbing a. 방해가 되는

_____ _____

어 · 휘 · 연 · 구

▶ 외우면서 단어를 2번씩 써보세요!

22 **co-ed** [kou éd]

a. 남녀공학의 n. 남녀공학

▶ allowing boys and girls to learn together

_____ _____

23 **play** [plei]

n. 연극, 희곡

▶ an acting performance

_____ _____

24 **serenade** [sèrənéid]

v. 세레나데를 부르다

▶ to sing a song to a person

_____ _____

25 **disappointed** [dìsəpóintid]

a. 실망한

▶ a little sad and upset

▷ disappoint v. 실망시키다

▷ disappointment n. 실망

_____ _____

26 **supervisor** [súːpərvàizər]

n. 감독관

▶ a person who ensures other people behave correctly

▷ supervision n. 감독

_____ _____

27 **rotate** [róuteit]

v. 교대하다

▶ to take turns doing a job

▷ rotation n. 교대

_____ _____

28 **match** [mætʃ]

n. 어울리는 짝

▶ a partner, someone you are compatible with

_____ _____

Exercise

A 주어진 뜻에 해당하는 단어를 보기에서 찾아 쓰세요.

> praise   faculty   prestigious   accommodate   responsibility
> guideline   college   dormitory   competent   assess

① a place where students study to get a qualification like a university _____
② well-known, important and admired _____
③ to provide for, to supply with food, housing, etc. _____
④ to compliment and say nice things about something _____
⑤ having ability, talents, and skills _____
⑥ the staff of a college or university _____
⑦ a set of rules and instructions that tell someone how to behave _____
⑧ a duty that someone has because of their job or position _____
⑨ to test, to evaluate _____
⑩ a place where students live on campus _____

B 단어의 관계에 맞게 빈칸을 채우세요.

① rotate : _____ = 교대하다 : 교대
② tolerate : tolerance = 견디다 : _____
③ _____ : advice = 신입생지도 교수 : 충고
④ praise : _____ = 칭찬 : 칭찬할 만한
⑤ assess : _____ = 평가하다 : 평가
⑥ luxurious : luxury = 호화스러운 : _____
⑦ laundry : do laundry = 빨래 : _____
⑧ _____ : disturb = 방해 : 방해하다

C 의미가 같도록 알맞은 단어를 넣어 문장을 완성하세요.

1. You can climb a ladder to the girls' dormitory if you find a perfect _____.
   이상적인 상대를 발견하면 여학생 기숙사에 사다리를 놓고 올라갈 수 있잖아요.

2. There are _____ in the girls' dormitory.
   여학생 기숙사에는 감독관이 있어.

3. My uncle seemed to be _____ that the dormitories were separate.
   우리 삼촌은 기숙사가 분리되었다는 것에 대해 실망하는 것처럼 보였어.

4. Romeo looked up at Juliet's window and _____ her.
   로미오는 줄리엣의 창문을 올려다보면서 그녀에게 세레나데를 불러주었어.

5. It reminded me of the _____, Romeo and Juliet.
   그건 나에게 로미오와 줄리엣이라는 연극을 상기시켰어.

6. Although the school was _____, the girls' dormitory was separate.
   그 학교는 남녀공학이었지만, 여학생 기숙사는 분리되어 있었어.

7. There was a _____ on the first floor.
   1층에는 빨래방이 있었어.

8. Don't they _____ time off to play?
   그들은 나가서 놀 시간을 가질 만하지 않니?

D 녹음된 내용을 듣고, 다음 빈칸에 들어갈 단어나 표현을 쓰세요.

Dear Diary,

My uncle is a _____ student. • He gained admission to a _____ college. • It has the best _____ in Korea. • After the entrance ceremony, there was an _____ for freshmen. • Students and guests _____ in the auditorium. • It was big enough to _____ about 5,000 people. • The principal praisedthe students. • He said how _____ they were.

Then he introduced the _____ members. • After that, he explained the _____ of campus life. • Then the school _____ came on stage. • She said being a college student is a big _____. • She explained how they _____ students and she talked about how important _____ _____ are. • Whew, three years of cramming and studying? • How do students _____ it? • Don't they _____ time off to play? • After the ceremony, we went to the _____ where my uncle will stay. • It didn't look very _____. • There was a _____ on the first floor. • Students can do _____ there. • There were signs on the doors of some rooms that said "Do not make _____." • Although the school was co-ed, the girls' dormitory was _____. • It reminded me of the _____, Romeo and Juliet. • Romeo looked up at Juliet's window and _____ her. • My uncle seemed to be _____ that the dormitories were separate. • There are _____ in the girls' dormitory. • They _____ their shifts every night. • Don't be disappointed, uncle. • You can climb a ladder to the girls'dormitory if you find a perfect _____.

▶ 1단계 : 먼저 그림을 보고, 이 장의 에피소드를 추측해 보세요.

→ enrich one's mind

→ order not to violate one's freedom of speech

Dear Mom,

I read an article about my favorite band, the Volcanoes. ● It really aroused anger in me. ● It says they won't be on TV for some time and this stirs me. ● Some officials made a decision to censor the band. ● They said there are some problems with the contents of some songs. ● They said their songs are uneducational. ● They claim the songs will ruin students. ● They seem to think that the Volcanoes are criminals. ● What an outdated idea! ● What criteria did they use to decide this? ● I'm in a rage.

Undoubtedly, they don't know what art is. ● Mom, you said it's an absurd decision. ● Their songs enrich my mind. ● You said we live in a democracy. ● In a democracy, people have a right to free speech. ● But what's happening here? ● Mom, you checked my text messages. ● You can't deny it. ● Hoony is my witness. ● Mom, are you going to betray your own beliefs? ● I want you to be objective. ● Are you trying to confine me? ● When you check my messages, you violate my freedom of speech. ● Even prisoners have a right to say what they want. ● If I were a judge, I would order you not to do this. ● You're not allowed to touch my phone. ● Any objections, mom?

1 **article** [ɑ́ːrtikl]

n. 기사

▶ a piece of writing in a newspaper or magazine

_____ _____

2 **arouse** [əráuz]

v. 자극하다

▶ to bring about or cause a feeling or idea in someone

_____ _____

3 **stir** [stəːr]

v. 감정을 자극하다

▶ to make a person react with strong emotions
▶ stirring a. (감정을) 자극하는

_____ _____

4 **censor** [sénsər]

v. 검열하다

▶ to edit or cover up parts of something (art, music, etc.)
▶ censorship n. 검열

_____ _____

5 **content** [kəntént]

n. 내용

▶ substance or ideas in songs or books

_____ _____

6 **uneducational**

[ənèdʒukéiʃənəl]

a. 비교육적인

▶ not educational, having no educational value

_____ _____

7 **ruin** [rúːin]

v. 망치다 n. 파멸

▶ to damage or spoil something
▶ ruination n. 파괴, 황폐
▶ ruinous a. 파괴된, 황폐한

_____ _____

어·휘·연·구

▶ 외우면서 단어를 2번씩 써보세요!

8 criminal [krímənəl]

n. 범죄자

▶ a person who commits crimes and breaks laws
▶ crime n. 범죄

_____   _____

9 outdated [áutdéitid]

a. 시대에 뒤떨어진

▶ not modern and not useful, obsolete

_____   _____

10 criterion [kraitíəriən]

n. 기준, 표준

▶ a set of beliefs that someone uses to judge how good or bad
▶ something is; a standard
▶ criteria (criterion의 복수형)

_____   _____

11 rage [reidʒ]

n. 성냄, 분노

▶ strong anger, explosion
▶ in a rage 화가 난

_____   _____

12 undoubtedly [Àndáutidli]

ad. 의심할 여지 없이

▶ definitely, surely, certainly

_____   _____

13 absurd [əbsə́:rd]

a. 불합리한, 어리석은

▶ stupid, silly, foolish, not logical

_____   _____

14 enrich [enrítʃ]

v. 풍부하게 하다

▶ to improve something, to make it better
▶ enrichment n. 풍부하게 함

_____   _____

15 democracy [dimάkrəsi]
n. 민주주의
▶ a society where everybody has the same rights
▶ democrat n. 민주주의자
▶ democratic a. 민주주의의

_____ _____

16 free speech [fri: spi:tʃ]
언론의 자유
▶ the right that people can say what they want

_____ _____

17 check [tʃek]
v. 확인하다
▶ to look at something to make sure it is correct

_____ _____

18 deny [dinάi]
v. 부인하다
▶ to say something is not true
▶ denial n. 부인

_____ _____

19 witness [wítnis]
n. 목격자 v. 목격하다
▶ a person who sees something and tells about it

_____ _____

20 betray [bitréi]
v. 배신하다, 등지다
▶ to say or do something against one's beliefs
▶ betrayal n. 배신

_____ _____

21 objective [əbdʒéktiv]
a. 객관적인 n. 목표, 목적
▶ making good and fair decisions
▶ objectivity n. 객관성

_____ _____

▶ 외우면서 단어를 2번씩 써보세요!

22 confine [kənfáin]

v. 가두다, 제한하다

▶ to imprison; to limit someone, to stop someone doing a particular activity

▶ confinement n. 감금, 제한

_____ _____

23 violate [váiəléit]

v. 침해하다, 위반하다

▶ to disturb someone's privacy or peace; to do something against someone's rights; to break a law or rule

▶ violation n. 침해, 위반

_____ _____

24 prisoner [príznər]

n. 죄수

▶ a criminal who has broken the law and is in prison

_____ _____

25 judge [dʒʌdʒ]

n. 판사 v. 판단하다

▶ a person who decides how a criminal will be punished

▶ judgment n. 판단

_____ _____

26 allow [əláu]

v. 허락하다

▶ to let someone do something, to give permission

_____ _____

27 objection [əbdʒékʃən]

n. 반대

▶ disagreement, counter-agreement

▶ object v. 반대하다

▶ objective n. 목적 a. 객관적인

▶ objectionable a. 반대할 만한

_____ _____

Exercise

A 주어진 뜻에 해당하는 단어를 보기에서 찾아 쓰세요.

> undoubtedly　article　fresh speech　uneducational　outdated
> democracy　check　content　arouse　absurd

① a piece of writing in a newspaper or magazine _____
② to bring about or cause a feeling or idea in someone _____
③ substance or ideas in songs or books _____
④ not educational, having no educational value _____
⑤ not modern and not useful, obsolete _____
⑥ definitely, surely, certainly _____
⑦ stupid, silly, foolish, not logical _____
⑧ a society where everybody has the same rights _____
⑨ the right that people can say what they want _____
⑩ to look at something to make sure it is correct _____

B 단어의 관계에 맞게 빈칸을 채우세요.

① object : objective = 반대하다 : _____
② Judge : _____ = 판사 : 판단
③ betray : _____ = 배신하다 : 배신
④ _____ : denial = 부인하다 : 부인
⑤ rage : _____ = 성냄 : 화가 난
⑥ criminal : _____ = 범죄자 : 범죄
⑦ _____ : censorship = 검열하다 : 검열
⑧ ruin : ruination = 망치다 : _____

C 의미가 같도록 알맞은 단어를 넣어 문장을 완성하세요.

1. I read an _____ about my favorite band, the Volcanoes.
   저는 제가 좋아하는 밴드인 볼케이노에 대한 기사를 읽었어요.

2. It says they won't be on TV for some time and this _____ me.
   그들이 한동안 텔레비전에 나오지 않을 거라고 쓰여 있고 그것이 저의 감정을 자극해요.

3. They said there are some problems with the _____ of some songs.
   그들은 노래 몇 개의 내용에 문제가 있다고 말했어요.

4. What an _____ idea!
   정말 시대에 뒤떨어진 생각이에요!

5. You're not _____ to touch my phone.
   엄마는 제 전화를 만질 수 없어요.

6. Even _____ have a right to say what they want.
   죄수들조차도 자신이 원하는 것을 말할 권리가 있어요.

7. Are you trying to _____ me?
   저를 가두려고 하시는 건가요?

8. Hoony is my _____.
   후니가 증인이에요.

D 녹음된 내용을 듣고, 다음 빈칸에 들어갈 단어나 표현을 쓰세요.

Dear Mom,

I read an _____ about my favorite band, the Volcanoes. ● It really _____ anger in me. ● It says they won't be on TV for some time and this _____ me. ● Some officials made a decision to _____ the band. ● They said there are some problems with the _____ of some songs. ● They said their songs are _____. ● They claim the songs will _____ students. ● They seem to think that the Volcanoes are _____. ● What an _____ idea! ● What _____ did they use to decide this? ● I'm in a _____.

_____, they don't know what art is. ● Mom, you said it's an _____ decision. ● Their songs _____ my mind. ● You said we live in a _____. ● In a democracy, people have a right to _____ _____. ● But what's happening here? ● Mom, you _____ my text messages. ● You can't _____ it. ● Hoony is my _____. ● Mom, are you going to _____ your own beliefs? ● I want you to be _____. ● Are you trying to _____ me? ● When you check my messages, you violate my freedom of speech. ● Even _____ have a right to say what they want. ● If I were a _____, I would order you not to do this. ● You're not _____ to touch my phone. ● Any _____, mom? ●

■ 녹음을 듣고, 해당하는 단어와 뜻을 쓰세요.

1	단어:	뜻:	2	단어:	뜻:
3	단어:	뜻:	4	단어:	뜻:
5	단어:	뜻:	6	단어:	뜻:
7	단어:	뜻:	8	단어:	뜻:
9	단어:	뜻:	10	단어:	뜻:
11	단어:	뜻:	12	단어:	뜻:
13	단어:	뜻:	14	단어:	뜻:
15	단어:	뜻:	16	단어:	뜻:
17	단어:	뜻:	18	단어:	뜻:
19	단어:	뜻:	20	단어:	뜻:
21	단어:	뜻:	22	단어:	뜻:
23	단어:	뜻:	24	단어:	뜻:
25	단어:	뜻:	26	단어:	뜻:
27	단어:	뜻:	28	단어:	뜻:
29	단어:	뜻:	30	단어:	뜻:

Voca Plus

복수형 −s와 접두사 ex−

복수형 −s가 명사 뒤에 붙어서 전혀 다른 뜻의 단어를 만들기도 한다. ex−는 'former'라는 뜻의 접두사로, '전에 어떤 지위나 신분에 있었던 자'를 뜻하는 단어를 만든다.

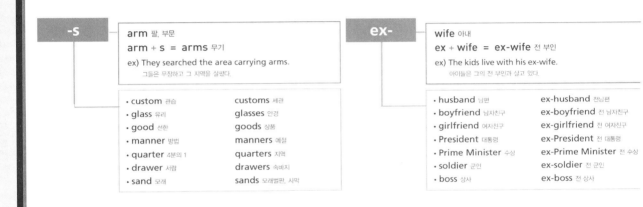

−s

arm 팔, 부문
arm + s = arms 무기
ex) They searched the area carrying arms.
　　그들은 무장하고 그 지역을 살폈다.

• custom 관습	customs 세관
• glass 유리	glasses 안경
• good 선한	goods 상품
• manner 방법	manners 예절
• quarter 4분의 1	quarters 지역
• drawer 서랍	drawers 속바지
• sand 모래	sands 모래벌판, 사막

ex−

wife 아내
ex + wife = ex-wife 전 부인
ex) The kids live with his ex-wife.
　　아이들은 그의 전 부인과 살고 있다.

• husband 남편	ex-husband 전남편
• boyfriend 남자친구	ex-boyfriend 전 남자친구
• girlfriend 여자친구	ex-girlfriend 전 여자친구
• President 대통령	ex-President 전 대통령
• Prime Minister 수상	ex-Prime Minister 전 수상
• soldier 군인	ex-soldier 전 군인
• boss 상사	ex-boss 전 상사

Culture Plus

Court 재판

+ **plaintiff** 원고　　　　+ **defendant** 피고

+ **jury** 배심원

+ **appeal** 상소

+ **verdict** 판결

+ **testify** 증언하다

+ **constitution** 헌법

+ **file a lawsuit** 제소하다

Chapter 4

Trips and Entertainment

▶ 1단계 : 먼저 그림을 보고, 이 장의 에피소드를 추측해 보세요.

→ **maintain primitive traditions and ceremonies** ●

● **be bewildered** ←

→ **become accustomed to a lifestyle** ●

Dear Diary,

Why do people try climbing to the peaks of mountains? ● I recently watched a program featuring a movie star. ● He climbed to the summit of a mountain in the Himalayas. ● What motivated him? ● I thought about what his ultimate goal could have been. ● Maybe he wanted to test his limits. ● It made me wonder, "Can we survive in a primitive society?" ● I also watched a show where a man visited a tribe in the Amazon. ● It was an uncivilized society. ● They were like real barbarians. ● However, they had an orderly society. ● They still maintained primitive traditions and ceremonies. ● For example, they worshiped crocodiles. ● On special days, their priest held ceremonies. ● They thought the ceremonies would drive away evil spirits. ● They seemed very superstitious. ● A few other things that surprised me were how precious fire was and that bugs were edible to them. ● When they asked the man to eat bugs, he was bewildered. ● Surprisingly, these people have keen senses and they use their instincts to hunt. ● They sharpen sticks to make them into arrows. ● With arrows, they hunt for food and protect themselves from predators. ● After hunting, they have a big celebration. ● They distribute food among each other. ● They try to maintain equality among the whole tribe. ● At the end of the program, the man seemed to have become accustomed to this primitive lifestyle. ● I wonder, "Where's the border between civilization and barbarism?" ● It seems difficult to draw a boundary between them.

▶ 3단계 : 외우면서 단어를 2번씩 써보세요!

1 peak [pi:k]
n. 정상
▶ the highest level, top of something

_____   _____

2 feature [fíːtʃər]
v. 특집으로 다루다 n. 특별기사, 특징
▶ to give special attention to

_____   _____

3 summit [sʌ́mit]
n. 정상
▶ the highest point or part as of a hill

_____   _____

4 motivate [móutəvèit]
v. 동기부여하다, 자극하다
▶ to provide incentive for action
▶ motivation n. 동기부여, 자극
▶ motive n. 동기 a. 움직이게 하는

_____   _____

5 ultimate [ʌ́ltəmit]
a. 궁극적인
▶ final, last
▶ ultimately ad. 마침내

_____   _____

6 limit [límit]
n. 한계 v. 한정하다
▶ the final, utmost, or furthest boundary

_____   _____

7 survive [sərváiv]
v. 살아남다
▶ to remain alive, to continue to live
▶ survival n. 생존 ▶ survivor n. 생존자

_____   _____

8 tribe [traib]
n. 부족
▶ a local division of an aboriginal people

_____   _____

9 **uncivilized** [ʌ̀nsívəlàizd]
a. 미개한
▶ not civilized or cultured; barbarous

_____   _____

10 **barbarian** [bɑːrbɛ́əriən]
n. 미개인, 야만인
▶ a person considered to have a primitive civilization
▶ barbarism n. 미개, 야만
▶ barbarous a. 야만스러운

_____   _____

11 **orderly** [ɔ́ːrdərli]
a. 규율이 있는
▶ organized, opposite of chaotic
▶ order n. 질서, 규율

_____   _____

12 **primitive** [prímətiv]
a. 원시적인, 초기의
▶ of an early state of human development

_____   _____

13 **worship** [wə́ːrʃip]
v. 숭배하다 n. 숭배, 예배
▶ to pay homage to God or any sacred object

_____   _____

14 **priest** [priːst]
n. 사제
▶ a person who performs religious rites, shaman, or holy person

_____   _____

15 **spirit** [spírit]
n. 영혼
▶ a ghost or supernatural being

_____   _____

▶ 3단계 : 외우면서 단어를 2번씩 써보세요!

16 superstitious [sùːpərstíʃəs]

a. 미신적인

▶ believing in supernatural beings
▶ superstition n. 미신

_____   _____

17 precious [préʃəs]

a. 귀중한

▶ valuable, important

_____   _____

18 edible [édəbəl]

a. 먹을 수 있는

▶ able to be consumed or eaten,
   eatable

_____   _____

19 bewildered [biwíldərd]

a. 당황한

▶ puzzled or confused
▶ bewilder v. 당황스럽게 하다
▶ bewilderment n. 당황스러움

_____   _____

20 keen [kiːn]

a. 예리한

▶ extremely sensitive or responsive

_____   _____

21 instinct [ínstiŋkt]

n. 본능

▶ an innate capability or aptitude,
   natural skill

_____   _____

22 sharpen [ʃáːrpən]

v. 날카롭게 하다

▶ to make or become sharp or sharper
▶ sharp a. 날카로운

_____   _____

▶ 외우면서 단어를 2번씩 써보세요!

㉓ predator [prédətər]
n. 침략자, 약탈자
▶ animals that hunt other animals for food; predatory people or organizations
▶ predatory a. 약탈하는

㉔ distribute [distríbjuːt]
v. 나누다, 분배하다
▶ to share things among the members of a group, to hand or deliver things
▶ distribution n. 분배
▶ distributor n. 분배자

㉕ equality [i(ː)kwáləti]
n. 평등
▶ the quality of being equal
▶ equal a. 평등한

㉖ accustomed [əkʌ́stəmd]
a. 적응이 된, 익숙한
▶ adjusted, experienced
▶ accustom v. ~을 적응시키다
▶ become accustomed to ~에 익숙해지다

㉗ border [bɔ́ːrdər]
n. 경계
▶ the line that separates one province from another

㉘ boundary [báundəri]
n. 경계선
▶ an imaginary line that separates one from another border

Exercise

A 주어진 뜻에 해당하는 단어를 보기에서 찾아 쓰세요.

> spirit   limit   tribe   worship   summit
> uncivilized   primitive   priest   peak   feature

① a the highest level, top of something _____
② to give special attention to _____
③ the highest point or part as of a hill _____
④ the final, utmost, or furthest boundary _____
⑤ a local division of an aboriginal people _____
⑥ not civilized or cultured; barbarous _____
⑦ of an early state of human development _____
⑧ to to pay homage to God or any sacred object _____
⑨ a person who performs religious rites, shaman, or holy person _____
⑩ a ghost or supernatural being _____

B 단어의 관계에 맞게 빈칸을 채우세요.

① survive : _____ = 살아남다 : 생존
② _____ : order = 규율이 있는 : 규율
③ _____ : equal = 평등 : 평등한
④ _____ : predatory = 침략자 : 약탈하는
⑤ sharp : _____ = 날카로운 : 날카롭게 하다
⑥ bewildered : _____ = 당황한 : 당황스럽게하다
⑦ motive : motivate = 동기 : _____
⑧ ultimate : ultimately = 궁극적인 : _____

C 의미가 같도록 알맞은 단어를 넣어 문장을 완성하세요.

1. It seems difficult to draw a _____ between them.
   둘 사이의 경계선을 표시하는 것은 어려울 것 같아.

2. I wonder, "Where's the _____ between civilization and barbarism?"
   나는 궁금해. "문명과 미개의 경계는 어디일까?"

3. They _____ food among each other.
   그들은 음식을 서로에게 나누어 줘.

4. Surprisingly, these people have keen senses and they use their_____to hunt.
   놀랍게도, 이 사람들은 예리한 감각을 가지고 있으며 사냥할 때 본능을 사용해.

5. They seemed very _____.
   그들은 매우 미신적인 것처럼 보였어.

6. They were like real _____.
   그들은 진짜 미개인 같았어.

7. Maybe he wanted to test his _____.
   아마 그는 자신의 한계를 시험하고 싶었을지도 몰라.

8. He climbed to the _____ of a mountain in the Himalayas.
   그는 히말라야 산맥에 있는 어떤 산의 정상에 올랐어.

D 녹음된 내용을 듣고, 다음 빈칸에 들어갈 단어나 표현을 쓰세요.

Dear Diary,

Why do people try climbing to the _____ of mountains? ● I recently watched a program _____ a movie star. ● He climbed to the _____ of a mountain in the Himalayas. ● What _____ him? ● I thought about what his _____ goal could have been. ● Maybe he wanted to test his _____. ● It made me wonder, "Can we _____ in a primitive society?" ● I also watched a show where a man visited a _____ in the Amazon. ● It was an _____ society. ● They were like real _____. ● However, they had an _____ society. ● They still maintained _____ traditions and ceremonies. ● For example, they _____ crocodiles. ● On special days, their _____ held ceremonies. ● They thought the ceremonies would drive away evil _____. ● They seemed very _____. ● A few other things that surprised me were how _____ fire was and that bugs were _____ to them. ● When they asked the man to eat bugs, he was _____. ● Surprisingly, these people have _____ senses and they use their _____ to hunt. ● They _____ sticks to make them into arrows. ● With arrows, they hunt for food and protect themselves from _____. ● After hunting, they have a big celebration. ● They _____ food among each other. ● They try to maintain _____ among the whole tribe. ● At the end of the program, the man seemed to have become _____ to this primitive lifestyle. ● I wonder, "Where's the _____ between civilization and barbarism?" ● It seems difficult to draw a _____ between them.

▶ 1단계 : 먼저 그림을 보고, 이 장의 에피소드를 추측해 보세요.

→ disguise oneself as a Santa Claus ●

→ volunteer and visit an orphanage ●

Dear Yuni,

Yuni, what are you going to do on Christmas Eve? ● Dongjin ordered us to check everything. ● Isn't he like a dictator? ● He's always barking out commands. ● Anyway, we're supposed to visit an orphanage. ● We're going to volunteer there. ● You need to collect games, CDs, and some toys, too. ● Otherwise, the kids will be dissatisfied. ● We also have some food being donated. ● It's lucky those anonymous donors gave us so much stuff. ● Thanks to them, this won't cost too much. ● I'm going to disguise myself as a Santa Claus. ● I'll wear loose pants and a fake beard and I'll exaggerate my voice. ● Yuni, are you going to assist me as a reindeer? ● Jungho has been designated as the coordinator. ● He is going to arrange the show. ● He'll organize the whole process. ● But who is going to entertain them? ● You recommend Jisu? ● I think her music skills are superior to anyone else I know. ● What else do we need to confirm before the event? ● After we finish there, we are going to go to a nursing home. ● Do you know what senior citizens like? ● My grandma really likes sweets and humorous stories. ● I have to confess that I'm good at making people laugh. ● I can improvise interesting stories. ● Our only obstacle is we don't have a car. ● Can you ask your mom to lend us her jeep?

어·휘·연·구

1 **order** [ɔ́:rdər]

v. 명령하다, 지시하다 n. 명령

▶ to give an order, direction, or command

---

2 **dictator** [díkteitər]

n. 독재자

▶ an absolute ruler, an undemocratic leader, a tyrant
▶ dictate v. 명령하다
▶ dictatorial a. 독재자의

---

3 **command** [kəmǽnd]

n. 명령 v. 명령하다

▶ an order given with authority

---

4 **orphanage** [ɔ́:rfənidʒ]

n. 고아원

▶ an institution for the housing and care of orphans
▶ orphan n. 고아

---

5 **volunteer** [váləntíər]

v. 자원봉사하다 n. 자원봉사자

▶ to do something without being forced to do it

---

6 **collect** [kəlékt]

v. 모으다

▶ to gather something together, to assemble
▶ collection n. 수집

---

7 **dissatisfied** [dissǽtisfàid]

a. 불만스러운

▶ not contented, disappointed
▶ dissatisfy v. 불만을 느끼게 하다
▶ dissatisfaction n. 불만, 불평

▶ 외우면서 단어를 2번씩 써보세요!

8 **donate** [dóuneit]
v. 기부하다
▶ to present as a gift, grant, or contribution
▷ donation n. 기부

_____ _____

9 **donor** [dóunər]
n. 기부자
▶ someone who makes a donation

_____ _____

10 **cost** [kɔːst]
v. 돈이 들다 n. 비용
▶ to require the payment of money
▷ costly a. 값비싼

_____ _____

11 **disguise** [disgáiz]
v. 변장하다 n. 변장
▶ to change one's appearance or identity

_____ _____

12 **loose** [luːs]
a. 헐렁한
▶ big, baggy, opposite of tight

_____ _____

13 **exaggerate** [igzǽdʒərèit]
v. 과장하다
▶ to overstate, to embellish
▷ exaggeration n. 과장
▷ exaggerated a. 과장된

_____ _____

14 **assist** [əsíst]
v. 돕다
▶ to give aid or help
▷ assistant n. 조수
▷ assistance n. 조력, 원조

_____ _____

15 designate [dézignèit]
v. 지명하다, 선정하다
▶ to choose someone to do a particular job
▶ designation n. 임명, 지정

16 arrange [əréindʒ]
v. 준비하다, 예정을 세우다
▶ to prepare or plan
▶ arrangement n. 정열, 정리

17 process [práses]
n. 과정
▶ a systematic series of actions directed to some end

18 entertain [èntərtéin]
v. 즐겁게 하다
▶ to amuse, to captivate
▶ entertainment n. 오락
▶ entertaining a. 재미있는

19 recommend [rèkəménd]
v. 추천하다
▶ to suggest, to represent something as positive
▶ recommendation n. 추천

20 superior [səpíəriər]
a. 뛰어난
▶ higher in rank or importance, opposite of inferior
▶ superior to ~보다 뛰어난

21 confirm [kənfɔ́:rm]
v. 확인하다
▶ to establish the truth, to verify
▶ confirmation n. 확인

▶ 외우면서 단어를 2번씩 써보세요!

22 nursing home [nə́ːrsiŋ houm]
양로원
▶ a place where elderly and sickly people live and are taken care of

_____ _____

23 senior citizen [síːjər sítəzə]
노인
▶ an elderly person

_____ _____

24 humorous [hjúːmərəs]
a. 우스운, 재미있는
▶ funny, having a good sense of humor
▶ humor n. 유머, 익살

_____ _____

25 confess [kənfés]
v. 고백하다, 인정하다
▶ to admit that something is true
▶ confession n. 고백

_____ _____

26 improvise [ímprəvàiz]
v. 즉흥적으로 만들다
▶ to make something without planning
▶ improvisation n. 즉석에서 하기

_____ _____

27 obstacle [ábstəkəl]
n. 장애물
▶ something preventing someone from continuing

_____ _____

28 lend [lend]
v. 빌려주다
▶ to allow someone to borrow something

_____ _____

Exercise

A 주어진 뜻에 해당하는 단어를 보기에서 찾아 쓰세요.

volunteer	exaggerate	recommend	disguise	loose
order	process	donor	command	entertain

① to give an order, direction, or command _____
② an order given with authority _____
③ to do something without being forced to do it _____
④ someone who makes a donation _____
⑤ to change one's appearance or identity _____
⑥ big, baggy, opposite of tight _____
⑦ to overstate, to embellish _____
⑧ a systematic series of actions directed to some end _____
⑨ to amuse, to captivate _____
⑩ to suggest, to represent something as positive _____

B 단어의 관계에 맞게 빈칸을 채우세요.

① dictator : dictate = 독재자 : _____
② _____ : orphan = 고아원 : 고아
③ collect : _____ = 모으다 : 수집
④ dissatisfied : _____ = 불만스러운 : 불만을 느끼게 하다
⑤ donate : _____ = 기부하다 : 기부
⑥ cost : costly = 돈이 들다 : _____
⑦ assistant : assist = _____ : 돕다
⑧ _____ : humor = 우스운 : 익살

C 의미가 같도록 알맞은 단어를 넣어 문장을 완성하세요.

1. Can you ask your mom to _____ us her jeep?
   엄마한테 지프를 빌려달라고 부탁할 수 있니?

2. Our only _____ is we don't have a car.
   우리의 유일한 장애물은 우리는 차가 없다는 거야.

3. I can _____ interesting stories.
   나는 즉흥적으로 재미있는 이야기를 만들 수 있어.

4. I have to _____ that I'm good at making people laugh.
   나는 사람들을 웃게 만드는 재주가 있다는 걸 고백해야겠다.

5. Do you know what _____ like?
   노인들이 무엇을 좋아하는지 알고 있니?

6. After we finish there, we are going to go to a
   그곳에서 행사가 끝난 후에, 우리는 요양원으로 갈 거야.

7. What else do we need to _____ before the event?
   행사 전에 우리는 그 외에 무엇을 확인해야 하지?

8. You _____ Jisu?
   너는 지수를 추천하는 거니?

D 녹음된 내용을 듣고, 다음 빈칸에 들어갈 단어나 표현을 쓰세요.

Dear Yuni,

Yuni, what are you going to do on Christmas Eve? ● Dongjin _____ us to check everything. ● Isn't he like a _____? ● He's always barking out _____. ● Anyway, we're supposed to visit an _____. ● We're going to _____ there. ● You need to _____ games, CDs, and some toys, too. ● Otherwise, the kids will be _____. ● We also have some food being _____. ● It's lucky those anonymous _____ gave us so much stuff. ● Thanks to them, this won't _____ too much. ● I'm going to _____ myself as a Santa Claus. ● I'll wear _____ pants and a fake beard and I'll _____ my voice. ● Yuni, are you going to _____ me as a reindeer? ● Jungho has been _____ as the coordinator. ● He is going to _____ the show. ● He'll organize the whole _____. ● But who is going to _____ them? ● You _____ Jisu? ● I think her music skills are _____ to anyone else I know. ● What else do we need to _____ before the event? ● After we finish there, we are going to go to a nursing home. ● Do you know what _____ _____ like? ● My grandma really likes sweets and _____ stories. ● I have to _____ that I'm good at making people laugh. ● I can _____ interesting stories. ● Our only _____ is we don't have a car. ● Can you ask your mom to _____ us her jeep?

▶ 1단계 : 먼저 그림을 보고, 이 장의 에피소드를 추측해 보세요.

→ **perform the commencement**

score a goal ←

→ **translate English for parents**

Episode

Sara seems to adjust well. ● Here is an e-mail from her.

Dear Bomi,

Hey, Bomi, our community is holding a special event. ● It's a biannual event. ● The city council sponsors it. ● I met people from various ethnic backgrounds. ● At the end, there was a final football match and a party. ● Traditionally, there is an intense rivalry between the two teams, the Lions and the Bears. ● Before the match, a man performed the commencement. ● He also poured beer into a soccer ball-shaped trophy. ● I felt as if I was watching a commercial. ● Players on both teams made an oath. ● They looked serious. ● They looked solemn. ● They reminded me of warriors. ● They were there as a delegation from each community. ● Carlos, a player from our team, scored two goals. ● His play was unmatchable. ● His skills were sophisticated. ● While watching him play, the people were in awe. ● People praised him as if he were a legendary soccer player. ● His opponents could not touch him. ● In the second half, Carlos proceeded to continue his excellent play. ● He scored another goal and the people applauded. ● The spectators were overwhelmed. ● After the game, there was a multinational party. ● People prepared a variety of food. ● I was able to meet people who spoke English with various accents. ● And I translated it for my parents.

1 **adjust** [ədʒʌ́st]

v. 적응하다

▶ to adapt, to change depending on one's environment

▶ adjustment n. 적응

▶ adjustable a. 적응할 수 있는

_____   _____

2 **community** [kəmjúːnəti]

n. 지역사회

▶ neighborhood

_____   _____

3 **biannual** [baiǽnjuəl]

a. 1년에 두 번의

▶ occurring twice a year

_____   _____

4 **sponsor** [spánsər]

v. 후원하다 n. 후원, 후원자

▶ to provide money to pay for an event

_____   _____

5 **ethnic** [éθnik]

a. 민족의, 인종의

▶ having to do with a particular race or ethnicity

▶ ethnicity n. 민족성

_____   _____

6 **final** [fáinəl]

a. 결승의

▶ last, ultimate, end

▶ finalize v. 완성시키다, 끝내다

_____   _____

7 **rivalry** [ráivəlri]

n. 경쟁

▶ intense competition between two teams

▶ rival v. 경쟁하다 n. 경쟁자 a. 경쟁하는

_____   _____

▶ 외우면서 단어를 2번씩 써보세요!

8 **commencement**
[kəménsmənt]
n. 개회식, 시작
▶ a ceremony for the start of an event
▶ commence v. 시작하다

_____ _____

9 **shaped** [ʃeipt]
a. ~모양을 한
▶ in the form of, having the same form or shape
▶ shape v. 형태를 취하다 n. 모양

_____ _____

10 **commercial** [kəmə́ːrʃəl]
n. 상업광고 a. 상업상의
▶ an advertisement, a show for advertising products
▶ commerce n. 상업

_____ _____

11 **oath** [ouθ]
n. 선서
▶ a promise, a contract
▶ make an oath 선서를 하다

_____ _____

12 **serious** [síəriəs]
a. 진지한
▶ determined, without humor
▶ seriousness n. 진지함

_____ _____

13 **solemn** [sáləm]
a. 엄숙한
▶ quiet, serious

_____ _____

14 **warrior** [wɔ́(ː)riər]
n. 전사
▶ a fighter, a soldier

_____ _____

▶ 3단계 : 외우면서 단어를 2번씩 써보세요!

15 delegation [dèligéiʃən]
n. 대표단
▶ a group of people in charge of representing people
▶ delegate v. 파견하다, 위임하다 n. 대표

_____ _____

16 score [skɔːr]
v. 득점하다
▶ to make a goal, to gain a point or goal

_____ _____

17 unmatchable [ʌnmǽtʃəbəl]
a. 대항할 수 없는
▶ unbeatable, incomparable in skill or strength

_____ _____

18 sophisticated [səfístəkèitid]
a. 정교한
▶ experienced, refined, well-developed
▶ sophisticate v. 궤변을 부리다 n. 세련된 사람

_____ _____

19 awe [ɔː]
n. 경외, 경외심
▶ admiration, astonishment
▶ in awe 경외하여

_____ _____

20 legendary [lédʒəndèri]
a. 전설의
▶ fabulous, unreal, unforgettable
▶ legend n. 전설

_____ _____

21 opponent [əpóunənt]
n. 적수, 상대
▶ the other team or person you are playing against

_____ _____

▶ 외우면서 단어를 2번씩 써보세요!

22 proceed [prousíːd]

v. 나아가다, 진행하다

▶ to continue, to progress
▶ process n. 진행, 진전
▶ procedure n. 절차, 진행

_____   _____

23 applaud [əplɔ́ːd]

v. 박수치다, 칭찬하다

▶ to cheer, to clap
▶ applause n. 박수

_____   _____

24 spectator [spékteitər]

n. 관중

▶ audience

_____   _____

25 multinational [mÀltinǽʃənəl]

a. 다국적의

▶ multiethnic, having many nationalities

_____   _____

26 variety [vəràiəti]

n. 다양성

▶ many different kinds or types
▶ various a. 다양한
▶ a variety of 다양한

_____   _____

27 accent [ǽksent]

n. 악센트

▶ a different pronunciation, different sound

_____   _____

28 translate [trænsléit]

v. 통역하다

▶ to interpret, to change one language to another
▶ translation n. 통역
▶ translator n. 통역자

_____   _____

Exercise

A 주어진 뜻에 해당하는 단어를 보기에서 찾아 쓰세요.

> opponent   sponsor   warrior oath   score   biannual
> unmatchable   solemn   sophisticated   community

① neighborhood _____
② occurring twice a year _____
③ to provide money to pay for an event _____
④ a promise, a contract _____
⑤ quiet, serious _____
⑥ a fighter, a soldier _____
⑦ to make a goal, to gain a point or goal _____
⑧ unbeatable, incomparable in skill or strength _____
⑨ experienced, refined, well-developed _____
⑩ the other team or person you are playing against _____

B 단어의 관계에 맞게 빈칸을 채우세요.

① ethnic : _____ = 민족의 : 민족성
② final : finalize = 결승의 : _____
③ _____ : rival = 경쟁 : 경쟁하다
④ _____ : shape = ~ 모양을 한 : 모양
⑤ awe : in awe = 경외 : _____
⑥ legendary : _____ = 전설의 : 전설
⑦ proceed : process = _____ : 진행
⑧ _____ : various = 다양성 : 다양한

C 의미가 같도록 알맞은 단어를 넣어 문장을 완성하세요.

1. And I _____ it for my parents.
   그리고 나는 부모님을 위해 통역했어.

2. I was able to meet people who spoke English with various _____.
   나는 다양한 악센트로 영어를 말하는 사람들을 만날 수 있었어

3. After the game, there was a _____ party.
   게임이 끝난 후에, 다국적 파티가 열렸어.

4. The _____ were overwhelmed.
   관중들은 압도되었어.

5. He scored another goal and the people _____.
   그는 또 한 골을 넣었고 사람들은 환호했어

6. His _____ could not touch him.
   그의 적들은 그와는 상대할 수가 없었어.

7. His skills were _____.
   그의 기술은 정교했어.

8. His play was _____.
   그의 경기는 대항할 수 없는 것이었어.

D 녹음된 내용을 듣고, 다음 빈칸에 들어갈 단어나 표현을 쓰세요.

Sara seems to _____ well. ● Here is an e-mail from her.

Dear Bomi,

Hey, Bomi, our _____ is holding a special event. ● It's a _____ event. ● The city council _____ it. ● I met people from various _____ backgrounds. ● At the end, there was a _____ football match and a party. ● Traditionally, there is an intense _____ between the two teams, the Lions and the Bears. ● Before the match, a man performed the _____. ● He also poured beer into a soccer ball-_____ trophy. ● I felt as if I was watching a _____. ● Players on both teams made an _____. ● They looked _____. ● They looked _____. ● They reminded me of _____. ● They were there as a _____ from each community. ● Carlos, a player from our team, _____ two goals. ● His play was _____. ● His skills were _____. ● While watching him play, the people were in ____. ● People praised him as if he were a _____ soccer player. ● His _____ could not touch him. ● In the second half, Carlos _____ to continue his excellent play. ● He scored another goal and the people _____. ● The _____ were overwhelmed. ● After the game, there was a _____ party. ● People prepared a _____ of food. ● I was able to meet people who spoke English with various _____. ● And I _____ it for my parents.

Test (Unit 10~Unit 12)

■ 녹음을 듣고, 해당하는 단어와 뜻을 쓰세요.

1	단어:	뜻:	2	단어:	뜻:
3	단어:	뜻:	4	단어:	뜻:
5	단어:	뜻:	6	단어:	뜻:
7	단어:	뜻:	8	단어:	뜻:
9	단어:	뜻:	10	단어:	뜻:
11	단어:	뜻:	12	단어:	뜻:
13	단어:	뜻:	14	단어:	뜻:
15	단어:	뜻:	16	단어:	뜻:
17	단어:	뜻:	18	단어:	뜻:
19	단어:	뜻:	20	단어:	뜻:
21	단어:	뜻:	22	단어:	뜻:
23	단어:	뜻:	24	단어:	뜻:
25	단어:	뜻:	26	단어:	뜻:
27	단어:	뜻:	28	단어:	뜻:
29	단어:	뜻:	30	단어:	뜻:

Voca Plus

접두사 bi- / mono-

bi-는 'two'라는 뜻의 접두사로, '둘(한 쌍) 또는 이중'이라는 뜻의 단어를 만든다.
mono-는 'one'이라는 뜻의 접두사로, '단일'이라는 뜻의 단어를 만든다.

bi-

weekly 매주
bi + weekly = biweekly 격주의
ex) Starting next month, the newsletter will be
printed biweekly.
다음 달부터 회보가 격주로 출간될 겁니다.

- **annual** 해마다의
- **centennial** 100년마다의
- **-cycle** 바퀴
- **lateral** 측면의
- **lingual** 언어의
- **-gamy** 결합
- **partisan** 당파적인

- **biannual** 연 2회의, 반년마다의
- **bicentennial** 200년마다의
- **bicycle** 자전거
- **bilateral** 양면이 있는
- **bilingual** 2개 국어의
- **bigamy** 중혼죄
- **bipartisan** 두 정당의

mono-

rail 궤도
mono + rail = monorail 모노레일, 단궤 철도
ex) You can take the monorail to the pier.
부두까지 모노레일을 타고 갈 수 있습니다.

- **-logue** 담화, 연설
- **-gamy** 결합
- **-chrome** 색소
- **syllable** 음절
- **tone** 음조
- **molecular** 분자의
- **lingual** 언어의

- **monologue** 독백
- **monogamy** 일부일처
- **monochrome** 단색화, 흑백사진
- **monosyllable** 단음절
- **monotone** 단조
- **monomolecular** 한 분자의
- **monolingual** 1개의 언어를 사용하는

Culture Plus

Sports Game   운동 경기

+ **referee** 심판

+ **spectator** 관중

+ **amateur** 아마추어

+ **professional** 프로 선수

+ **preliminary game** 예선 경기

+ **final game** 본선 경기

+ **tournament** 선수권 대회

VOCA EDGE

Chapter 5

Hobbies

▶ 1단계 : 먼저 그림을 보고, 이 장의 에피소드를 추측해 보세요.

→ **listen to meditation music**

demonstrate some postures ←

→ **stretch one's legs**

Episode

▶ 2단계 : 녹음 내용을 들으며, 추측한 에피소드와 비교해 보세요.

Bomi: Mom, what's this music for? ● It's so monotonous. ● Why don't you listen to lively music?

Mom: Bomi, it's meditation music. ● It's good for mental health. ● It's also good for purifying our minds.

Bomi: Mom, you're not a Buddhist monk.

Mom: You don't know the real value of it.

Bomi: Do you think it's good for relieving stress? ● Hip-hop music is a better option for stress relief.

My mom registered for yoga class. ● Listening to meditation music is one of her routines. ● She says yoga benefits us. ● She emphasizes its health benefits. ● Before she started yoga classes she had an ulcer, but now she's okay. ● This made me recall a similar thing. ● Mom once said tea has healing effects. ● Now she stays healthy doing yoga. ● My mom says it's good for enlightening people. ● She also says it gives insight into life and it helps control our emotions. ● She really admires people who are good at yoga. ● This morning she demonstrated some unusual postures. ● She also made me stretch my legs.

Bomi: Ouch, it's torture. ● Mom, I can't maintain this posture. ● Don't press my shoulders.

Mom: Bomi, you need more tenacity. ● These exercises are effective in strengthening organs.

Bomi: Okay, mom. ● I will try, but my body is too stiff.

▶ 3단계 : 외우면서 단어를 2번씩 써보세요!

1 monotonous [mənátənəs]
a. 단조로운
▶ boring and repetitive
▶ monotone n. 단조 a. 단조의
▶ monotony n. 단조로움

_____   _____

2 lively [láivli]
a. 경쾌한
▶ dynamic and full of energy
▶ liveliness n. 경쾌함

_____   _____

3 meditation [mèdətéiʃən]
n. 명상
▶ being in a quiet, calm state
▶ meditate v. 명상하다, 숙고하다
▶ meditative a. 명상적인, 심사숙고하는

_____   _____

4 mental [méntl]
a. 정신의
▶ relating to one's mind
▶ mentality n. 지력

_____   _____

5 purify [pjúərəfài]
v. 정화하다
▶ to make something clean, to remove any bad things
▶ purification n. 정화
▶ pure a. 순수한

_____   _____

6 Buddhist [búːdist]
n. 불교도
▶ a member of the Buddhist religion
▶ Buddhism n. 불교

_____   _____

7 value [vǽljuː]
n. 가치
▶ how much something is worth
▶ valuable a. 귀중한
▶ invaluable a. 매우 귀중한
▶ valueless a. 가치가 없는

_____   _____

▶ 외우면서 단어를 2번씩 써보세요!

8 **relieve** [rilí:v]

v. 줄이다

▶ to make an unpleasant feeling less
▶ relief n. 경감

_____   _____

9 **option** [ápʃən]

n. 선택

▶ a choice

_____   _____

10 **register** [rédʒəstər]

v. 등록하다

▶ to join a class
▶ registration n. 등록

_____   _____

11 **routine** [ru:tí:n]

n. 일과

▶ an activity someone does on a regular basis

_____   _____

12 **benefit** [bénəfit]

v. 이익을 주다 n. 이익

▶ to be good for someone
▶ beneficial a. 이로운

_____   _____

13 **emphasize** [émfəsàiz]

v. 강조하다

▶ to strongly tell one's opinion to someone
▶ emphasis n. 강조

_____   _____

14 **ulcer** [ʌ́lsər]

n. 궤양

▶ a painful sore, often inside one's stomach

_____   _____

15 **recall** [rikɔ́:l]

v. 생각나게 하다, 상기시키다

▶ to remember

_____   _____

16 **healing** [híːliŋ]
a. 치료하는
▶ making someone better and healthy
▶ heal v. 치료하다

_____ _____

17 **enlighten** [enláitn]
v. 가르치다, 계몽시키다
▶ to cause someone to understand, to civilize someone
▶ enlightenment n. 계몽

_____ _____

18 **insight** [ínsàit]
n. 통찰력
▶ accurate and deep understanding
▶ insightful a. 통찰력 있는

_____ _____

19 **emotion** [imóuʃən]
n. 감정
▶ feelings such as love, anger, happiness, etc.
▶ emotional a. 감정적인

_____ _____

20 **admire** [ædmáiər]
v. 동경하다, 감탄하다
▶ to like and respect someone or something
▶ admiration n. 감탄
▶ admirable a. 감탄할 만한

_____ _____

21 **demonstrate** [démənstrèit]
v. 시범을 보이다
▶ to show someone how to do something
▶ demonstration n. 시범, 실연

_____ _____

▶ 외우면서 단어를 2번씩 써보세요!

22 stretch [stretʃ]

v. 뻗다

▶ to push one's arms or legs away from one's body
▶ stretchy a. 신축성 있는

_____ _____

23 torture [tɔ́:rtʃər]

n. 고문

▶ something which causes pain
▶ torturous a. 고통스러운

_____ _____

24 maintain [meintéin]

v. 유지하다

▶ to continue doing something
▶ maintenance n. 유지

_____ _____

25 press [pres]

v. 누르다

▶ to push something

_____ _____

26 tenacity [tənǽsəti]

n. 끈기

▶ diligence, firmness, perseverance
▶ tenacious a. 끈기 있는

_____ _____

27 strengthen [stréŋkθən]

v. 강화하다

▶ to make someone or something stronger
▶ strength n. 힘
▶ strengthening a. 강화시키는

_____ _____

28 stiff [stif]

a. 뻣뻣한

▶ firm or not easily bent
▶ stiffen v. 근육 등이 경직되다

_____ _____

Exercise

A 주어진 뜻에 해당하는 단어를 보기에서 찾아 쓰세요.

| press | recall | enlighten | lively | option | ulcer |
| monotonous | Buddhist | register | routine | | |

① a choice   _____
② an activity someone does on a regular basis   _____
③ a painful sore, often inside one's stomach   _____
④ to remember   _____
⑤ to cause someone to understand, to civilize someone   _____
⑥ to push something   _____
⑦ boring and repetitive   _____
⑧ dynamic and full of energy   _____
⑨ a member of the Buddhist religion   _____
⑩ to join a class   _____

B 단어의 관계에 맞게 빈칸을 채우세요.

① stiff : stiffen = 뻣뻣한 : _____
② _____ : heal = 치료하는 : 치료하다
③ emotion : _____ = 감정 : 감정적인
④ mental : mentality = 정신의 : _____
⑤ purify : pure = 정화하다 : _____
⑥ value : _____ = 가치 : 귀중한
⑦ relieve : relief = 줄이다 : _____
⑧ _____ : emphasis = 강조하다 : 강조

C 의미가 같도록 알맞은 단어를 넣어 문장을 완성하세요.

1. These exercises are effective in _____ organs.
   이 운동은 사람의 장기를 강화하는 데 효과가 있어.

2. Bomi, you need more _____.
   보미, 좀 더 끈기가 있어야겠구나

3. Don't _____ my shoulders.
   제 어깨를 누르지 마세요.

4. Mom, I can't _____ this posture.
   엄마, 저는 이 자세를 유지할 수 없어요.

5. Ouch, it's _____.
   아야, 이건 고문이에요

6. She also made me _____ my legs.
   그녀는 나보고 다리를 뻗어보라고 시키기도 하셨다.

7. This made me _____ a similar thing.
   이것 때문에 나는 비슷한 것을 생각하게 되었다.

8. She really _____ people who are good at yoga.
   그녀는 요가에 정통한 사람들을 정말 동경하신다.

D 녹음된 내용을 듣고, 다음 빈칸에 들어갈 단어나 표현을 쓰세요.

Bomi: Mom, what's this music for? ● It's so _____. ● Why don't you listen
to _____ music?

Mom: Bomi, it's _____ music. ● It's good for _____ health. ● It's also good
for _____ our minds.

Bomi: Mom, you're not a _____ monk.

Mom: You don't know the real _____ of it.

Bomi: Do you think it's good for _____ stress? ● Hip-hop music is a better
_____ for stress relief.

My mom _____ for yoga class. ● Listening to meditation music is one of her
_____. ● She says yoga _____ us. ● She _____ its health benefits.
● Before she started yoga classes she had an _____, but now she's okay. ● This
made me _____ a similar thing. ● Mom once said tea has _____ effects. ●
Now she stays healthy doing yoga. ● My mom says it's good for _____
people. ● She also says it gives _____ into life and it helps control our
_____. ● She really _____ people who are good at yoga. ● This morning
she _____ some unusual postures. ● She also made me _____ my legs.

Bomi: Ouch, it's _____. ● Mom, I can't _____ this posture. ● Don't _____
my shoulders.

Mom: Bomi, you need more _____. ● These exercises are effective in
_____ organs.

Bomi: Okay, mom. ● I will try, but my body is too _____.

Chapter 5 Hobbies

▶ 1단계 : 먼저 그림을 보고, 이 장의 에피소드를 추측해 보세요.

→ **have no right to say no**

be exclusively open to someone ←

→ **justify one's behavior**

Episode

▶ 2단계 : 녹음 내용을 들으며, 추측한 에피소드와 비교해 보세요.

Dear Diary,

Today we had a rehearsal for the play, "A Midsummer Night's Dream." • The seniors gave me some difficult tasks. • Bomi, can you move this equipment downstairs? • Are they insane? • How can I carry such heavy things? • But I can't reject them. • It's obligatory to follow their orders. • I have no right to say no. • Why are they so inconsiderate? • How come thoughtful seniors have this kind of attitude? • Right before a performance, we receive special training. • There is tension between juniors and seniors. • All seniors become very strict and our relationship becomes like that of employees and employer. • Usually juniors are not allowed to enter the seniors' meeting room. • The meeting room is like a room for executives. • It is exclusively open to seniors. • They create a hierarchy between us. • The seniors monitor everything. • We need to get permission to do things. • We can't ask for pay or leave. • There is no paternity leave or maternity leave. • We literally become slaves. • Bomi, vacuum the floor. Be quick. • Okay, Bomi, be flexible, I said to myself. • You might think my reaction is too passive. • It's true I have an inner conflict about this. • The seniors always justify their behavior, saying it's for a better performance. • In two years, I will get the same privilege. • So I'm not so pessimistic about my future.

▶ 3단계 : 외우면서 단어를 2번씩 써보세요!

1 **rehearsal** [rihə́:rsəl]
n. 예행연습
▶ a practice of a play or music in preparation for a performance
▶ rehearse v. 예행연습하다

_____ _____

2 **equipment** [ikwípmənt]
n. 장비
▶ things that someone uses to do a task

_____ _____

3 **insane** [inséin]
a. 미친
▶ crazy
▶ insanity n. 실성

_____ _____

4 **reject** [ridʒékt]
v. 거절하다
▶ to say no, not to accept a proposal, a request, or an offer
▶ rejection n. 거절

_____ _____

5 **obligatory** [əblígətɔ̀:ri]
a. 의무적인
▶ necessary, compulsory, mandatory
▶ oblige v. 강요하다
▶ obligation n. 의무

_____ _____

6 **right** [rait]
n. 권리
▶ authority to do something
▶ have a right to + V ~할 권리가 있다

_____ _____

7 **inconsiderate** [ìnkənsídərit]
a. 인정 없는
▶ careless, not caring about another person's feelings
▶ considerate a. 사려 깊은

_____ _____

▶ 외우면서 단어를 2번씩 써보세요!

8 **thoughtful** [θɔ́:tfəl]
a. 사려 깊은
▶ being careful of another person's feelings, considerate

_____ _____

9 **training** [tréiniŋ]
n. 훈련
▶ preparation, discipline
▶ train v. 훈련하다
▶ trainee n. 훈련생

_____ _____

10 **tension** [ténʃən]
n. 긴장감, 긴장
▶ an uncomfortable feeling
▶ tense a. 긴장한

_____ _____

11 **senior** [sí:jər]
n. 선배
▶ someone who is older or has more power than you
▶ seniority n. 손위임, 손위

_____ _____

12 **employer** [emplɔ́iər]
n. 고용주
▶ a person who hires someone to do a job
▶ employee n. 고용인

_____ _____

13 **junior** [dʒú:njər]
n. 후배
▶ someone who is younger and has less power than you

_____ _____

14 **executive** [igzékjətiv]
n. 중역
▶ a powerful businessman

_____ _____

15 exclusively [iksklú:sivli]
ad. 배타적으로
▶ available to only one person or one group
▶ exclusive a. 배타적인, 독점적인

_____ _____

16 hierarchy [háiərà:rki]
n. 계급제
▶ a system of separating people into different levels, grouping
▶ hierarchical a. 계급제의

_____ _____

17 monitor [mánitər]
v. 감시하다
▶ to supervise, to watch people carefully

_____ _____

18 permission [pə:rmíʃən]
n. 허가
▶ agreement, approval, consent
▶ permit v. 허가하다

_____ _____

19 leave [li:v]
n. 휴가
▶ vacation time

_____ _____

20 maternity leave
[mətə́:rnəti li:v]
출산 휴가
▶ vacation time a mother is allowed to take off work when she gives birth
▶ maternity n. 모성, 모계
▶ maternal a. 어머니의
▶ paternity n. 부성, 부계
▶ paternal a. 아버지의

_____ _____

21 literally [lítərəli]
ad. 완전히, 글자 뜻대로
▶ completely, really, exactly
▶ literal a. 글자 그대로의

_____ _____

어·휘·연·구

22 vacuum [vǽkjuəm]
v. 진공청소기로 청소하다
▶ to clean the floor with a vacuum cleaner

_____ _____

23 flexible [fléksəbəl]
a. 융통성이 있는
▶ being adaptable, changing easily when a situation changes
▶ flexibility n. 융통성

_____ _____

24 passive [pǽsiv]
a. 수동적인
▶ quiet, not reacting aggressively
▶ passivity n. 수동성

_____ _____

25 conflict [kánflikt]
n. 갈등 v. 충돌하다
▶ serious disagreement and argument

_____ _____

26 justify [dʒʌ́stəfài]
v. 정당화하다
▶ to show that something is reasonable or necessary
▶ justification n. 정당화

_____ _____

27 privilege [prívəlidʒ]
n. 특권
▶ a special advantage that is given to some people
▶ privileged a. 특권이 있는

_____ _____

28 pessimistic [pésəmístik]
a. 비관적인
▶ expecting a bad outcome, cynical
▶ pessimism n. 비관론
▶ pessimist n. 비관론자

_____ _____

Exercise

A 주어진 뜻에 해당하는 단어를 보기에서 찾아 쓰세요.

equipment	reject	inconsiderate	thoughtful	employer
exclusively	monitor	vacuum	flexible	justify

① a person who hires someone to do a job _____
② careless, not caring about another person's feelings _____
③ to supervise, to watch people carefully _____
④ being adaptable, changing easily when a situation changes_____
⑤ to say no, not to accept a proposal, a request, or an offer _____
⑥ available to only one person or one group _____
⑦ to clean the floor with a vacuum cleaner _____
⑧ things that someone uses to do a task _____
⑨ to show that something is reasonable or necessary _____
⑩ being careful of another person's feelings, considerate _____

B 단어의 관계에 맞게 빈칸을 채우세요.

① rehearsal : rehearse = _____ : 예행연습하다
② insane : _____ = 미친 : 실성
③ training : _____ = 훈련 : 훈련생
④ tension : tense = 긴장감 : _____
⑤ hierarchy : hierarchical = 계급제 : _____
⑥ _____ : permit = 허가 : 허가하다
⑦ passive : _____ = 수동적인 : 수동성
⑧ privilege : privileged = _____ : 특권이 있는

C 의미가 같도록 알맞은 단어를 넣어 문장을 완성하세요.

1. It's _____ to follow their orders.
   그들의 명령을 따르는 것이 의무거든.

2. Usually_____are not allowed to enter the seniors' meeting room.
   보통 후배들은 선배들의 회의실에 들어갈 수 없어.

3. The meeting room is like a room for _____.
   회의실은 회사의 중역을 위한 방과 같은 거야.

4. There is no paternity leave or _____.
   아버지 출산 휴가나 어머니 출산 휴가는 없어.

5. We _____ become slaves.
   우리는 완전히 노예가 되어가고 있어.

6. It's true I have an inner _____ about this.
   나는 이 문제에 대해 마음 속에 갈등이 있는 게 사실이야.

7. In two years, I will get the same _____.
   2년 후에, 나도 같은 특권을 갖게 되겠지.

8. So I'm not so _____ about my future.
   그래서 나는 나의 미래에 대해 그렇게 비관적이지 않아.

D 녹음된 내용을 듣고, 다음 빈칸에 들어갈 단어나 표현을 쓰세요. 🎧

Dear Diary,

Today we had a _____ for the play, "A Midsummer Night's Dream." ● The seniors gave me some difficult tasks. ● Bomi, can you move this _____ downstairs? ● Are they _____? ● How can I carry such heavy things? ● But I can't _____ them. ● It's _____ to follow their orders. ● I have no _____ to say no. ● Why are they so _____? ● How come _____ seniors have this kind of attitude? ● Right before a performance, we receive special _____. ● There is _____ between juniors and seniors. ● All _____ become very strict and our relationship becomes like that of employees and _____. ● Usually _____ are not allowed to enter the seniors' meeting room. ● The meeting room is like a room for _____. ● It is _____ open to seniors. ● They create a _____ between us. ● The seniors _____ everything. ● We need to get _____ to do things. ● We can't ask for pay or _____. ● There is no paternity leave or maternity leave. ● We literally become slaves. ● Bomi, _____ the floor. Be quick. ● Okay, Bomi, be _____, I said to myself. ● You might think my reaction is too _____. ● It's true I have an inner _____ about this. ● The seniors always _____ their behavior, saying it's for a better performance. ● In two years, I will get the same _____. ● So I'm not so _____ about my future.

▶ 1단계 : 먼저 그림을 보고, 이 장의 에피소드를 추측해 보세요.

→ be obsessed with something

know how the barter system works ←

→ sign a contract

▶ 2단계 : 녹음 내용을 들으며, 추측한 에피소드와 비교해 보세요.

Bomi: Hoony, look. Your cards are everywhere. ● Please dispose of your cards.

Hoony: Don't worry. I know the best disposal method. ● Bomi, don't give me such a suspicious look.

For two months, Hoony purchased strange cards every day. ● He seemed to be obsessed with these useless things. ● When I asked him about it, he just grinned at me. ● What's your purpose for collecting these cards? ● Then he divulged his plan to me. ● He triumphantly pulled a video game out of his bag. ● He had exchanged his cards for his friend Brian's brand-new video game. ● Wow, he seems to know how the economy works. ● He knows how he can make a surplus. ● He's acquired the basic theory already. ● I mean, he knows how the barter system works. ● Hoony, what if Brian changes his mind? ● Hoony showed me a written document. ● He said they signed a contract. ● It states certain conditions. ● For example, the contract is valid until September 21st. ● Then the contract will expire. ● He must be a good negotiator. ● It seems it's too good a deal. ● How did he convince Brian to exchange his brand-new game for these old cards? ● How did he make such a profitable deal? ● He said he showed Brian a few samples of his cards and Brian really liked them. ● Hoony's homeschooling is really working out well. ● Our dad told Hoony to keep an account book. ● Dad taught him what expenditure and income mean. ● Hoony already knows how to spend money.

1 dispose [dispóuzd]
v. 처분하다
▶ to throw away
▶ disposable a. 일회용의
▶ dispose of ~을 처분하다

_____   _____

2 disposal [dispóuzəl]
n. 폐기
▶ a way to throw something away

_____   _____

3 suspicious [səspíʃəs]
a. 의심스러운
▶ not trusting someone, distrustful
▶ suspicion n. 의심

_____   _____

4 purchase [pə́:rtʃəs]
v. 사다 n. 구입
▶ to buy something

_____   _____

5 obsess [əbsés]
v. 사로잡다
▶ to think about something all the time
▶ obsession n. 강박관념
▶ be obsessed with ~에 사로잡히다

_____   _____

6 grin [grin]
v. 이를 드러내고 싱긋 웃다
▶ to smile widely and show one's teeth

_____   _____

7 purpose [pə́:rpəs]
n. 목적
▶ a reason or goal for doing something

_____   _____

▶ 외우면서 단어를 2번씩 써보세요!

8 **divulge** [diválʤ]
v. 누설하다, 폭로하다
▶ to tell a person something that was a secret

_____   _____

9 **triumphantly** [traiʌ́mfəntli]
ad. 의기양양해서
▶ happily, boastfully
▷ triumphant a. 의기양양한

_____   _____

10 **brand-new** [brænd nju:]
a. 아주 새로운
▶ completely new

_____   _____

11 **economy** [ikánəmi]
n. 경제
▶ the way that business is organized
▷ economic a. 경제의
▷ economical a. 경제적인, 절약이 되는

_____   _____

12 **surplus** [sə́ːrplʌs]
n. 흑자
▶ extra material balance, something extra, opposite of deficit

_____   _____

13 **acquire** [əkwáiər]
v. 습득하다
▶ to get or learn something
▷ acquisition n. 획득, 습득

_____   _____

14 **barter** [bɑ́ːrtər]
n. 물물교환 v. 물물교환하다
▶ exchange of goods for other goods

_____   _____

15 **document** [dákjəmənt]

n. 서류

▶ a piece of paper with writing on it
▶ documentation n. 문서 분류 시스템

_____ _____

16 **contract** [kántrækt]

n. 계약서, 계약

▶ a formal written agreement

_____ _____

17 **state** [steit]

v. 언급하다

▶ to say something in a formal way
▶ statement n. 언급

_____ _____

18 **valid** [vǽlid]

a. 유효한

▶ able to be used; legally or officially
  acceptable
▶ validate v. 유효하게 하다
▶ validity n. 유효함, 타당성

_____ _____

19 **expire** [ikspáiər]

v. 만기가 되다

▶ to come to an end
▶ expiry n. 만기

_____ _____

20 **negotiator** [nigóuʃièitər]

n. 협상가

▶ a person who bargains, a middleperson
▶ negotiate v. 협상하다
▶ negotiation n. 협상

_____ _____

▶ 외우면서 단어를 2번씩 써보세요!

21 deal [diːl]
n. 거래 v. 거래하다
▶ a bargain

_____   _____

22 convince [kənvíns]
v. 설득하다, 확신시키다
▶ to make someone agree with you
▶ conviction n. 확신
▶ convincing a. 설득력 있는

_____   _____

23 profitable [práfitəbəl]
a. 이익이 되는
▶ making a profit
▶ profit n. 이익

_____   _____

24 homeschooling [hóumskùːliŋ]
n. 자택 학습
▶ teaching a child at home instead
of at school
▶ homeschool v. 자택에서 교육하다

_____   _____

25 account [əkáunt]
n. 회계, 계산
▶ a detailed record of all the money
one earns and spends
▶ accountant n. 회계사

_____   _____

26 expenditure [ikspénditʃər]
n. 지출
▶ money that one spends to buy
things, opposite of income

_____   _____

Exercise

A 주어진 뜻에 해당하는 단어를 보기에서 찾아 쓰세요.

contract	purchase	divulge	disposal	grin
purpose	triumphantly	barter	brand-new	surplus

① a way to throw something away   _____
② to buy something   _____
③ to smile widely and show one's teeth   _____
④ a reason or goal for doing something   _____
⑤ to tell a person something that was a secret   _____
⑥ happily, boastfully   _____
⑦ completely new   _____
⑧ extra material balance, something extra, opposite of deficit   _____
⑨ exchange of goods for other goods   _____
⑩ to a formal written agreement   _____

B 단어의 관계에 맞게 빈칸을 채우세요.

① state : _____ = 언급하다 : 언급
② account : accountant = 회계 : _____
③ valid : _____ = 유효한 : 유효하게 하다
④ economy : _____ = 경제 : 경제의
⑤ _____ : expiry = 만기가 되다 : 만기
⑥ _____ : acquisition = 습득하다 : 습득
⑦ profitable : profit = _____ : 이익
⑧ obsess : obsession = 사로잡다 : _____

C 의미가 같도록 알맞은 단어를 넣어 문장을 완성하세요.

1. We want our _____.
   우리는 우리만의 사생활을 원해요.

2. We have our own _____ phones.
   우리는 개인 전화를 가지고 있어요.

3. Sometimes _____ comments can cause problems, though.
   때로는 무자비한 비판이 문제가 되기도 하지만요.

4. I'm talking about _____ teens like me.
   저와 같은 일반적인 십대에 대해 이야기하는 거예요.

5. We post images of _____ on our blogs.
   우리는 유명인의 이미지를 블로그에 올려요.

6. We often stand in front of the mirror _____ pimples on our faces.
   우리는 얼굴에 난 여드름을 짜면서 종종 거울 앞에 서 있죠.

7. Do you know what we like to do when we feel _____?
   우리가 스트레스를 받을 때 무엇을 하고 싶어하는지 아세요?

8. Tips like how to pretend to_____on our studies while sending text messages.
   문자 메시지를 보내면서 공부에 집중하는 척하는 방법과 같은 조언이죠.

D 녹음된 내용을 듣고, 다음 빈칸에 들어갈 단어나 표현을 쓰세요.

Bomi: Hoony, look. Your cards are everywhere. ● Please _____ of your cards.

Hoony: Don't worry. I know the best _____ method. ● Bomi, don't give me such a _____ look.

For two months, Hoony _____ strange cards every day. ● He seemed to be _____ with these useless things. ● When I asked him about it, he just _____ at me. ● What's your _____ for collecting these cards? ● Then he _____ his plan to me. ● He _____ pulled a video game out of his bag. ● He had exchanged his cards for his friend Brian's _____ video game. ● Wow, he seems to know how the _____ works. ● He knows how he can make a surplus. ● He's _____ the basic theory already. ● I mean, he knows how the _____ system works. ● Hoony, what if Brian changes his mind? ● Hoony showed me a written _____. ● He said they signed a _____. ● It _____ certain conditions. ● For example, the contract is _____ until September 21st. ● Then the contract will _____. ● He must be a good _____. ● It seems it's too good a _____. ● How did he _____ Brian to exchange his brand-new game for these old cards? ● How did he make such a _____ deal? ● He said he showed Brian a few samples of his cards and Brian really liked them. ● Hoony's _____ is really working out well. ● Our dad told Hoony to keep an _____ book. ● Dad taught him what _____ and income mean. ● Hoony already knows how to spend money.

Test (Unit 13~Unit 15)

■ 녹음을 듣고, 해당하는 단어와 뜻을 쓰세요.

1	단어:	뜻:		2	단어:	뜻:
3	단어:	뜻:		4	단어:	뜻:
5	단어:	뜻:		6	단어:	뜻:
7	단어:	뜻:		8	단어:	뜻:
9	단어:	뜻:		10	단어:	뜻:
11	단어:	뜻:		12	단어:	뜻:
13	단어:	뜻:		14	단어:	뜻:
15	단어:	뜻:		16	단어:	뜻:
17	단어:	뜻:		18	단어:	뜻:
19	단어:	뜻:		20	단어:	뜻:
21	단어:	뜻:		22	단어:	뜻:
23	단어:	뜻:		24	단어:	뜻:
25	단어:	뜻:		26	단어:	뜻:
27	단어:	뜻:		28	단어:	뜻:
29	단어:	뜻:		30	단어:	뜻:

Voca Plus

✚
접두사 anti- / contra-

anti-와 contra-는 둘 다 'against'라는 뜻의 접두사이다.
anti-는 '적대 또는 배척'이라는 뜻의 단어를 만들고,
contra-는 '역(逆) 또는 반대'라는 뜻의 단어를 만든다.

anti-

government 정부
anti + government = antigovernment 반 정부의
ex) Another antigovernment protest took place on
Saturday.
토요일에 또 다른 반 정부 시위가 발생했다.

- -biotic 생명의   antibiotic 항생 물질의
- aging 노화   anti-aging 노화 방지의
- septic 부패성의   antiseptic 살균의
- -pathy 감정   antipathy 반감
- -onym 단어, 이름   antonym 반의어
- freeze 결빙   antifreeze 부동액
- social 사회적인, 사교적인   antisocial 반 사회적인, 반 사교적인

contra-

seasonal 계절의
contra + seasonal = contraseasonal 시기에 벗어난, 계절에 벗어난
ex) The recent rise in corn prices is contraseasonal.
최근 옥수수 가격의 인상은 계절에 맞지 않다.

- contraband 금지품
- contraception 피임
- contradict 반박하다
- contraflow 역행, 역류
- contravene 위반 행위를 범하다
- contralateral 몸의 반대쪽에서 일어나는
- contraindicate (증후가 약에 대한) 금기를 나타내다

Culture Plus

Religion 종교

+ **Buddhism** 불교

+ **Christianity** 기독교

+ **Catholicism** 천주교

+ **Islamism** 이슬람교

+ **Judaism** 유대교

+ **Hinduism** 힌두교

+ **Atheism** 무신론

SMART

Level.5

VOCA EDGE

Chapter 6

Health

▶ 1단계 : 먼저 그림을 보고, 이 장의 에피소드를 추측해 보세요.

→ **taste bitter**

become a hostage ←

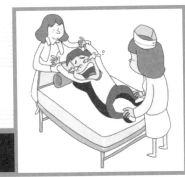

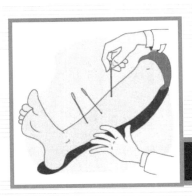

→ **stimulate blood circulation**

Bomi: Mom, are you going to see a physician for grandma? • And you are going to see a pediatrician for Hoony, right?

Mom: No, they're going to an oriental clinic with me.

Bomi: Do you mean an herbal doctor? • Hoony has a sprained ankle. • And grandma has high blood pressure. • Are you thinking of acupuncture?

Mom: Sure, it is good for their circulation.

Mom always says acupuncture stimulates blood circulation. • She seems to be addicted to acupuncture. • Once when I had food poisoning, she abruptly took me to the herbal clinic. • At the herbal clinic, the doctor took my pulse. • Then, can you just imagine? • I had to drink a black liquid. • At first glance, I could see that it was going to taste bitter. • I really wanted to stop, but it was compulsory. • Today Hoony is going to experience the same thing. • Mom says fear of needles is hereditary. • She says dad has a phobia of needles and so do Hoony and me. • But how can mom soothe him? • Won't he hesitate to enter the examination room? • He is going to cry frantically. • The nurse will hold him tightly and Hoony will become a hostage. • My poor brother, mom, you're inhumane. • Don't you think it's child abuse? • Why don't you acknowledge that I'm right?

1 **physician** [fizíʃən]
n. 내과의사
▶ a doctor

_____ _____

2 **pediatrician** [pìːdiətríʃənl]
n. 소아과 의사
▶ a doctor for children

_____ _____

3 **oriental** [ɔ̀ːriéntl]
a. 동양의
▶ having to do with Asian culture and/or history
▶ orient n. 동양

_____ _____

4 **herbal** [hə́rbəl]
a. 약초의, 식물의
▶ natural, made from plants and natural sources
▶ herb n. 허브, 약초

_____ _____

5 **sprained** [spreind]
a. 접지른, 삔
▶ having an injury of a joint
▶ sprain v. ~을 접지르다

_____ _____

6 **blood pressure** [blʌd préʃər]
혈압
▶ a measure of how strongly one's blood flows

_____ _____

7 **acupuncture** [ǽkjupʌ̀ŋktʃər]
n. 침술
▶ a type of medical treatment where needles are stuck into the body
▶ acupuncturist n. 침술사

_____ _____

▶ 외우면서 단어를 2번씩 써보세요!

⑧ circulation [sə̀:rkjəléiʃən]
n. 순환
▶ the flow of blood through one's body
▶ circulate v. 순환하다
▶ circular a. 원형의
▶ circulating a. 순환하는, 순회하는

_____   _____

⑨ stimulate [stímjəlèit]
v. 자극하다
▶ to arouse or cause to become active
▶ stimulation n. 자극

_____   _____

⑩ addicted [ədíktid]
a. 중독된
▶ hooked, unable to stop doing something
▶ addict v. 중독시키다 n. 중독자
▶ addiction n. 중독
▶ be addicted to ~에 중독되다

_____   _____

⑪ poisoning [pɔ́izəniŋ]
n. 중독
▶ a type of sickness caused by having a toxic substance in the body
▶ poison n. 독
▶ food poisoning n. 식중독

_____   _____

⑫ abruptly [əbrʌ́ptli]
ad. 갑작스럽게
▶ suddenly, hurriedly
▶ abrupt a. 갑작스런

_____   _____

⑬ pulse [pʌls]
n. 맥박
▶ heartbeat, the rate at which one's heart is beating

_____   _____

14 imagine [imǽdʒin]
v. 상상하다
▶ to think creatively
▶ imagination n. 상상
▶ imaginary a. 상상의
▶ imaginative a. 상상력이 풍부한

_____ _____

15 liquid [líkwid]
n. 액체
▶ a fluid, a state of matter between solid and gas

_____ _____

16 glance [glæns]
n. 흘긋 봄 v. 흘긋 보다
▶ looking quickly at something
▶ at first glance 첫눈에

_____ _____

17 compulsory [kəmpʌ́lsəri]
a. 강제적인, 의무의
▶ mandatory, necessary
▶ compulsion n. 강제
▶ compulsive a. 강박관념에 사로잡힌

_____ _____

18 experience [ikspíəriəns]
v. 경험하다 n. 경험
▶ to go through a situation or event
▶ experienced a. 경험이 있는

_____ _____

19 hereditary [hirédətèri]
a. 유전성의
▶ genetic, received from one's parents
▶ heredity n. 유전

_____ _____

20 phobia [fóubiə]
n. 공포증
▶ an intense fear of something
▶ phobic a. 공포증이 있는

_____ _____

어·휘·연·구

▶ 외우면서 단어를 2번씩 써보세요!

21 soothe [suːð]
v. 진정시키다
▶ to calm or relax someone or something
▶ soothing a. 진정시키는

_____ _____

22 hesitate [hézətèit]
v. 망설이다, 주저하다
▶ to wait a moment before acting, to act slowly because of uncertainty
▶ hesitation n. 망설임

_____ _____

23 frantically [fræntikəli]
ad. 미친 듯이
▶ wildly and uncontrollably
▶ frantic a. 미친

_____ _____

24 hostage [hástidʒ]
n. 인질
▶ a person being held

_____ _____

25 inhumane [ìnʰjuːméin]
a. 잔인한, 무자비한
▶ cruel, not ethical or caring
▶ inhumanity n. 무자비함, 비인간적임

_____ _____

26 abuse [əbjúːz]
n. 학대, 남용 v. 학대하다, 남용하다
▶ punishment or unethical physical treatment
▶ abusive a. 학대하는, 남용의

_____ _____

27 acknowledge [əknálidʒ]
v. 인정하다
▶ to accept or admit that something is true
▶ acknowledgement n. 승인, 인정

_____ _____

Exercise

A 주어진 뜻에 해당하는 단어를 보기에서 찾아 쓰세요.

> pediatrician acupuncture pulse glance hostage
> physician blood pressure stimulate imagine compulsory

① a doctor _____
② a doctor for children _____
③ a measure of how strongly one's blood flows _____
④ a type of medical treatment where needles are stuck into the body _____
⑤ to arouse or cause to become active _____
⑥ heartbeat, the rate at which one's heart is beating _____
⑦ a fluid, a state of matter between solid and gas _____
⑧ looking quickly at something _____
⑨ mandatory, necessary _____
⑩ a person being held _____

B 단어의 관계에 맞게 빈칸을 채우세요.

① abuse : _____ = 학대 : 학대하는
② frantically : _____ = 미친 듯이 : 미친
③ _____ : soothing = 진정시키다 : 진정시키는
④ _____ : phobic = 공포증 : 공포증이 있는
⑤ oriental : _____ = 동양의 : 동양
⑥ herbal : _____ = 약초의 : 약초
⑦ addict : addiction = 중독시키다 : _____
⑧ poisoning : poison = 중독 : _____

C 의미가 같도록 알맞은 단어를 넣어 문장을 완성하세요.

1. At the herbal clinic, the doctor took my _____.
   한의원에서, 의사는 내 맥박을 짚었다

2. Why don't you _____ that I'm right?
   제 말이 맞다고 인정하시는 것이 어떠세요?

3. My poor brother, mom, you're _____.
   불쌍한 내 동생. 엄마, 엄마는 잔인해요.

4. Won't he _____ to enter the examination room?
   그는 진료실에 들어가지 않으려고 하지 않을까?

5. Hoony has a _____ ankle.
   후니는 발목이 삐었어요.

6. Today Hoony is going to _____ the same thing.
   오늘은 후니가 같은 경험을 할 것이다

7. I had to drink a black _____.
   나는 검정색 액체를 마셔야 했다

8. Sure, it is good for their _____.
   물론이야, 그게 혈액순환에 좋거든.

D 녹음된 내용을 듣고, 다음 빈칸에 들어갈 단어나 표현을 쓰세요.

Bomi: Mom, are you going to see a _____ for grandma? ◦ And you are going to see a _____ for Hoony, right?

Mom: No, they're going to an _____ clinic with me.

Bomi: Do you mean an _____ doctor? ◦ Hoony has a _____ ankle. ◦ And grandma has high _____ _____. ◦ Are you thinking of _____?

Mom: Sure, it is good for their _____.

Mom always says acupuncture _____ blood circulation. ◦ She seems to be _____ to acupuncture. ◦ Once when I had food _____, she _____ took me to the herbal clinic. ◦ At the herbal clinic, the doctor took my _____. ◦ Then, can you just _____? ◦ I had to drink a black _____. ◦ At first _____, I could see that it was going to taste bitter. ◦ I really wanted to stop, but it was _____. ◦ Today Hoony is going to _____ the same thing. ◦ Mom says fear of needles is _____. ◦ She says dad has a _____ of needles and so do Hoony and me. ◦ But how can mom _____ him? ◦ Won't he _____ to enter the examination room? ◦ He is going to cry _____. ◦ The nurse will hold him tightly and Hoony will become a _____. ◦ My poor brother, mom, you're _____. ◦ Don't you think it's child _____? ◦ Why don't you _____ that I'm right?

▶ 1단계 : 먼저 그림을 보고, 이 장의 에피소드를 추측해 보세요.

→ be cautious when traveling

cope with emergencies ←

→ experiment on a dummy

Dear Sara,

Sara, is your friend okay now? ● I didn't know that rattle snakes were so poisonous. ● Your teacher was wise for taking prompt action. ● Otherwise he could have become paralyzed. ● He could have been in a critical condition. ● Sara, are there many casualties from snake bites in the desert? ● Tourists need to be cautious when traveling through deserts. ● Snakes there have natural camouflage. ● People can hardly distinguish between snakes and sand. ● Your video clips about that biologist surprised me. ● How could he just grab such lethal snakes? ● He even simultaneously explained about snakes while handling them. ● He seemed to ignore the fact that their poison could harm his nervous system. ● Or did he carry an antidote? ● In order to survive, we need to be able to cope with emergencies. ● They come to us unexpectedly. ● Today the whole class experimented on a dummy. ● We became a rescue team. ● Sara, suppose a little boy swallowed a small Lego block. ● His respiratory system wouldn't be able to function properly. ● Before he is sent to the emergency room, something must be done. ● Otherwise he will suffocate. ● Our teacher demonstrated some essential techniques to us. ● He showed us how to eliminate things blocking a person's airway. ● He also showed us how to inhale. ● We were also instructed to press on the dummy. ● "Hey, press on the chest not on the abdomen," teacher said to me. ● Playing with the dummy was not fun at all, but I will keep these instructions in mind. ● Who knows I may have to use them in the near future?

1 poisonous [pɔ́izənəs]
a. 독이 있는, 독성의
▶ causing poisoning, deadly, harmful
▶ poison n. 독

_____ _____

2 prompt [prɑmpt]
a. 신속한
▶ quick, done quickly, done right away
▶ promptly ad. 신속하게

_____ _____

3 paralyzed [pǽrəlàizd]
a. 마비된
▶ unable to move one's body
▶ paralyze v. 마비시키다
▶ paralysis n. 마비

_____ _____

4 critical [krítikəl]
a. 위독한, 위기의
▶ being in danger of death

_____ _____

5 casualty [kǽʒuəlti]
n. 사상자
▶ a person who is injured or killed in an incident

_____ _____

6 cautious [kɔ́ːʃəs]
a. 조심성 있는
▶ careful, not reckless
▶ caution n. 조심

_____ _____

7 camouflage [kǽmuflàːʒ]
n. 위장, 위장 수단
▶ disguise that keeps something hidden

_____ _____

▶ 외우면서 단어를 2번씩 써보세요!

8 **distinguish** [distíŋgwiʃ]
v. 구별하다
▶ to tell something apart from something different
▶ distinguished a. 구별되는

9 **biologist** [baiɑ́lədʒist]
n. 생물학자
▶ a person who specializes in biology
▶ biology n. 생물학

10 **lethal** [líːθəl]
a. 치명적인
▶ deadly, causing death

11 **simultaneously** [sàiməltéiniəsli]
ad. 동시에
▶ at the same time
▶ simultaneous a. 동시에 일어나는

12 **nervous system** [nɔ́ːrvəs sístəm]
신경계
▶ the system of the human body that controls organs

13 **antidote** [ǽntidòut]
n. 해독제
▶ anti-poison, a substance that can cure poison

14 **cope** [koup]
v. 대처하다, 극복하다
▶ o deal with, to attempt to overcome problems and difficulties
▶ cope with ~에 대처하다

▶ 3단계 : 외우면서 단어를 2번씩 써보세요!

15 unexpectedly [ʌ̀nikspéktədli]
ad. 갑자기
▶ surprisingly, abruptly

_____   _____

16 experiment [ikspérəmənt]
v. 실험하다 n. 실험
▶ to test or perform experiments

_____   _____

17 rescue [réskjuː]
n. 구조 v. 구조하다
▶ an attempt to save someone from
   a dangerous situation
▶ rescuer n. 구조하는 사람

_____   _____

18 swallow [swálou]
v. 삼키다
▶ to take something through the
   mouth and into the stomach

_____   _____

19 respiratory [réspərətɔ̀ːri]
a. 호흡의
▶ relating to breathing
▶ respiration n. 호흡
▶ respirator n. 인공호흡장치

_____   _____

20 emergency [imə́ːrdʒənsi]
n. 응급상황
▶ a situation that requires immediate
   help or assistance
▶ emergent a. 긴급한, 뜻밖의

_____   _____

21 suffocate [sʌ́fəkèit]
v. 질식하다, 질식시키다
▶ to die because of an inability to
   breathe
▶ suffocation n. 질식

_____   _____

▶ 외우면서 단어를 2번씩 써보세요!

22 essential [isénʃəl]
a. 필요한

▶ necessary, needed, required
▶ essence n. 본질, 요소

_____ _____

23 eliminate [ilímənèit]
v. 제거하다

▶ to get rid of, to remove
▶ elimination n. 제거

_____ _____

24 inhale [inhéil]
v. 숨을 들이쉬다

▶ to breath in

_____ _____

25 instruct [instrʌ́kt]
v. 지도하다

▶ to give information, to teach something
▶ instruction n. 지도
▶ instructive a. 교훈적인

_____ _____

26 abdomen [ǽbdəmən]
n. 복부

▶ part of the human body above the
waist and below the chest

_____ _____

27 keep in mind
[kiːp in maind]
기억해 두다

▶ to remember, to think about

_____ _____

Exercise

A 주어진 뜻에 해당하는 단어를 보기에서 찾아 쓰세요.

swallow	unexpectedly	nervous system	lethal	casualty
experiment	antidote	simultaneously	camouflage	critical

① being in danger of death _____
② a person who is injured or killed in an incident _____
③ disguise that keeps something hidden _____
④ deadly, causing death _____
⑤ at the same time _____
⑥ the system of the human body that controls organs _____
⑦ anti-poison, a substance that can cure poison _____
⑧ surprisingly, abruptly _____
⑨ to to test or perform experiments _____
⑩ to take something through the mouth and into the stomach _____

B 단어의 관계에 맞게 빈칸을 채우세요.

① instruct : _____ = 지도하다 : 지도
② eliminate : _____ = 제거하다 : 제거
③ essential : essence = 필요한 : _____
④ rescue : _____ = 구조 : 구조하는 사람
⑤ cope : _____ = 대처하다 : ~에 대처하다
⑥ _____ : biology = 생물학자 : 생물학
⑦ _____ : caution = 조심성 있는 : 조심
⑧ prompt : promptly = 신속한 : _____

C 의미가 같도록 알맞은 단어를 넣어 문장을 완성하세요.

1. Playing with the dummy was not fun at all, but I will_____these instructions_____.
   인체 모형을 가지고 노는 것은 전혀 재미가 없었지만, 나는 이 가르침을 기억할 거야.

2. "Hey, press on the chest not on the _____," teacher said to me.
   "이봐, 배가 아니라 가슴을 눌러" 선생님은 나에게 말씀하셨어.

3. He also showed us how to _____.
   그는 또한 숨을 들이쉬는 방법도 보여주셨어.

4. Otherwise he will _____.
   그렇지 않으면 그는 질식할 거야.

5. Before he is sent to the _____ room, something must be done.
   그가 응급실로 보내어지기 전에 뭔가 조치를 취해야 해.

6. His _____ system wouldn't be able to function properly.
   그의 호흡기관이 제대로 기능을 다 하지 못하게 될 거야.

7. They come to us _____.
   그런 상황은 우리에게 갑자기 오니까.

8. Or did he carry an _____?
   아니면 그는 해독제를 들고 다녔나?

D 녹음된 내용을 듣고, 다음 빈칸에 들어갈 단어나 표현을 쓰세요.

Dear Sara,

Sara, is your friend okay now? ● I didn't know that rattle snakes were so _____. ● Your teacher was wise for taking _____ action. ● Otherwise he could have become _____. ● He could have been in a _____ condition. ● Sara, are there many _____ from snake bites in the desert? ● Tourists need to be _____ when traveling through deserts. ● Snakes there have natural _____. ● People can hardly _____ between snakes and sand. ● Your video clips about that _____ surprised me. ● How could he just grab such _____ snakes? ● He even _____ explained about snakes while handling them. ● He seemed to ignore the fact that their poison could harm his _____ _____. ● Or did he carry an _____? ● In order to survive, we need to be able to _____ with emergencies. ● They come to us _____. ● Today the whole class _____ on a dummy. ● We became a _____ team. ● Sara, suppose a little boy _____ a small Lego block. ● His _____ system wouldn't be able to function properly. ● Before he is sent to the _____ room, something must be done. ● Otherwise he will _____. ● Our teacher demonstrated some _____ techniques to us. ● He showed us how to _____ things blocking a person's airway. ● He also showed us how to _____. ● We were also _____ to press on the dummy. ● "Hey, press on the chest not on the _____," teacher said to me. ● Playing with the dummy was not fun at all, but I will _____ these instructions _____ _____. ● Who knows I may have to use them in the near future?

Chapter

6 Health

▶ 1단계 : 먼저 그림을 보고, 이 장의 에피소드를 추측해 보세요.

→ **create antibodies**

● **combine exercise and laughter therapy** ←

→ **motivate someone to laugh**

Episode

Dear Diary,

Do you know how great laughter is? ● Laughter works like a miracle and its impact on life is great. ● Ha ha ha... My grandma's been combining exercise and laughter therapy for 2 months. ● Can you believe she once suffered from depression? ● Last year her close friend was diagnosed with Alzheimer's disease. ● After hearing the news, she lost her appetite. ● She even collapsed. ● The doctor said her bone density was decreasing. ● She said her hearing was deteriorating. ● She concluded that she was aging. ● She said that she didn't feel intellectual anymore. ● She wasn't willing to interact with anyone. ● But now, nothing can impede her. ● She is energetic and always motivates us to laugh. ● She tries to consume more vegetables than meat.

"Where is my anti-aging cream?" ● "Where is my sweatsuit?" ● "Can you give me a decaffeinated drink?" she says. ● Now all my family is sure that laughter creates antibodies. ● Her life expectancy should be increasing. ● Even her wrinkles seem to be gone. ● She doesn't even have to apply anti-aging cream on her face. ● Apparently laughter is the best medicine. ● Moreover it's contagious. ● So it affects us and spreads like an infectious disease. ● If you laugh, who wouldn't laugh along?

1 laughter [lǽftər]

n. 웃음

▶ the act of laughing
▶ laugh v. 웃다

_____   _____

2 miracle [mírəkəl]

n. 기적

▶ something amazing or unbelievable
▶ miraculous a. 기적의

_____   _____

3 impact [ímpækt]

n. 영향 v. 영향을 주다

▶ powerful effect or influence

_____   _____

4 combine [kəmbáin]

v. 결합하다

▶ to put one or more things together at the same time
▶ combination n. 조합

_____   _____

5 depression [dipréʃən]

n. 우울증

▶ a mental disease where a person is very sad
▶ depress v. ~을 우울하게 하다
▶ depressed a. 우울한

_____   _____

6 diagnose [dáiəgnòus]

v. 진단하다

▶ to recognize a disease by its signs and symptoms
▶ diagnosis n. 진단

_____   _____

7 appetite [ǽpitàit]

n. 식욕, 입맛

▶ desire to eat food
▶ appetizer n. 애피타이저

_____   _____

▶ 외우면서 단어를 2번씩 써보세요!

8 **collapse** [kəlǽps]
v. 쓰러지다
▶ to fall down completely.

_____ _____

9 **density** [dénsəti]
n. 밀도
▶ thickness, amount of mass per area
▶ dense a. 조밀한

_____ _____

10 **deteriorate** [ditíəriərèit]
v. 악화되다
▶ to become less in quality or amount, to gradually break down
▶ deterioration n. 악화
▶ deteriorating a. 악화되고 있는

_____ _____

11 **aging** [éidʒiŋ]
n. 나이 먹음, 노화
▶ the process of becoming older
▶ age v. 나이를 먹다, 늙다 n. 나이

_____ _____

12 **intellectual** [ìntəléktʃuəl]
a. 지적인 n. 지식인
▶ intelligent, able to think and reason well
▶ intellect n. 지성

_____ _____

13 **interact** [ìntərǽkt]
v. 상호작용하다
▶ to participate in actions with other people
▶ interaction n. 상호작용
▶ interactive a. 상호작용하는

_____ _____

14 **impede** [impíːd]
v. 방해하다, 지연시키다
▶ to prevent or disrupt the ability to do something
▶ impediment n. 방해, 지연

_____ _____

15 **energetic** [ènərdʒétik]
a. 활기에 찬
▶ having lots of energy and vigor
▶ energy n. 에너지

_____   _____

16 **motivate** [móutəvèit]
v. 동기부여하다, 자극하다
▶ to encourage, to provide a reason to act
▶ motivation n. 동기부여, 자극
▶ motive n. 동기 a. 움직이게 하는

_____   _____

17 **consume** [kənsú:m]
v. 먹다, 소비하다
▶ to eat or drink something
▶ consumption n. 소비

_____   _____

18 **anti-aging** [ǽnti éidʒiŋ]
a. 노화방지의
▶ slowing down the aging process

_____   _____

19 **sweatsuit** [swetù:t]
n. 운동복
▶ an outfit worn for exercise and activity

_____   _____

20 **decaffeinated**
[di:kǽfiənèitd]
a. 카페인이 없는
▶ not containing any caffeine

_____   _____

21 **antibody** [ǽntibád]
n. 항체
▶ part of one's body that fights against disease

_____   _____

▶ 외우면서 단어를 2번씩 써보세요!

22 life expectancy
[laif iklspéktənsi]
평균 수명
▶ how long a person is expected to live for

_____   _____

23 wrinkle [ríŋkəl]
n. 주름
▶ a line in the skin usually due to old age

_____   _____

24 apply [əplái]
v. 바르다, 적용하다
▶ to put something on, to use
▶ application n. (연고, 화장품 등을) 바름, 적용

_____   _____

25 apparently [əpǽrəntli]
ad. 분명히
▶ seemingly, outwardly
▶ apparent a. 명백한

_____   _____

26 contagious [kəntéidʒəs]
a. 전염성의
▶ spreading easily to cause similar action in others
▶ contagion n. 전염, 감염

_____   _____

27 infectious [infékʃəs]
a. 전염성의
▶ contagious, capable of spreading rapidly
▶ infect v. 전염시키다
▶ infection n. 전염, 감염

_____   _____

Exercise

A 주어진 뜻에 해당하는 단어를 보기에서 찾아 쓰세요.

wrinkle	impact	life expectancy	collapse	antibody
decaffeinated	deteriorate	sweatsuit	anti-aging	intellectual

① powerful effect or influence _____
② to fall down completely _____
③ to become less in quality or amount, to gradually break down _____
④ intelligent, able to think and reason well _____
⑤ slowing down the aging process _____
⑥ an outfit worn for exercise and activity _____
⑦ not containing any caffeine _____
⑧ part of one's body that fights against disease _____
⑨ how long a person is expected to live for _____
⑩ a line in the skin usually due to old age _____

B 단어의 관계에 맞게 빈칸을 채우세요.

① _____ : infect = 전염성의 : 전염시키다
② apparently : apparent = 분명히 : _____
③ motivate : _____ = 동기부여 하다 : 동기
④ energetic : energy = _____ : 에너지
⑤ _____ : interaction = 상호작용하다 : 상호작용
⑥ _____ : age = 노화 : 나이
⑦ density : dense = _____ : 조밀한
⑧ laughter : _____ = 웃음 : 웃다

C 의미가 같도록 알맞은 단어를 넣어 문장을 완성하세요.

1. Laughter works like a _____ and its impact on life is great.
   웃음은 기적과 같은 효과가 있고 인생에 미치는 영향은 대단해.

2. My grandma's been _____ exercise and laughter therapy for 2 months.
   우리 할머니는 운동과 웃음을 결합시킨 치료를 두 달 동안 받으셨어.

3. Can you believe she once suffered from _____?
   한때 그녀가 우울증에 시달렸다는 걸 믿을 수 있니?

4. Last year her close friend was _____ with Alzheimer's disease.
   작년에 그녀의 친한 친구분이 알츠하이머병이라는 진단을 받으셨어.

5. After hearing the news, she lost her _____.
   그 소식을 듣고 그녀는 입맛을 잃으셨어.

6. She said her hearing was _____.
   그녀는 청력도 악화되고 있다고 말씀하셨어.

7. But now, nothing can _____ her.
   그렇지만 지금은, 아무것도 그녀를 막을 수 없어.

8. She tries to _____ more vegetables than meat.
   그녀는 고기보다는 야채를 더 많이 드시려고 하셔.

D 녹음된 내용을 듣고, 다음 빈칸에 들어갈 단어나 표현을 쓰세요.

Dear Diary,

Do you know how great _____ is? ● Laughter works like a _____ and its _____ on life is great. ● Ha ha ha... My grandma's been _____ exercise and laughter therapy for 2 months. ● Can you believe she once suffered from _____? ● Last year her close friend was _____ with Alzheimer's disease. ● After hearing the news, she lost her _____. ● She even _____. ● The doctor said her bone _____ was decreasing. ● She said her hearing was _____. ● She concluded that she was _____. ● She said that she didn't feel _____ anymore. ● She wasn't willing to _____ with anyone. ● But now, nothing can _____ her. ● She is _____ and always _____ us to laugh. ● She tries to _____ more vegetables than meat.

"Where is my _____ cream?" ● "Where is my _____?" ● "Can you give me a _____ drink?" she says. ● Now all my family is sure that laughter creates _____. ● Her _____ _____ should be increasing. ● Even her _____ seem to be gone. ● She doesn't even have to _____ anti-aging cream on her face. ● _____ laughter is the best medicine. ● Moreover it's _____. ● So it affects us and spreads like an _____ disease. ● If you laugh, who wouldn't laugh along?

■ 녹음을 듣고, 해당하는 단어와 뜻을 쓰세요.

1	단어:	뜻:	2	단어:	뜻:
3	단어:	뜻:	4	단어:	뜻:
5	단어:	뜻:	6	단어:	뜻:
7	단어:	뜻:	8	단어:	뜻:
9	단어:	뜻:	10	단어:	뜻:
11	단어:	뜻:	12	단어:	뜻:
13	단어:	뜻:	14	단어:	뜻:
15	단어:	뜻:	16	단어:	뜻:
17	단어:	뜻:	18	단어:	뜻:
19	단어:	뜻:	20	단어:	뜻:
21	단어:	뜻:	22	단어:	뜻:
23	단어:	뜻:	24	단어:	뜻:
25	단어:	뜻:	26	단어:	뜻:
27	단어:	뜻:	28	단어:	뜻:
29	단어:	뜻:	30	단어:	뜻:

Voca Plus

접두사 ex- / in-

ex-는 'out'이라는 뜻의 접두사로, '~로부터,' '~밖으로'라는 뜻의 단어를 만든다.
in-은 'in'이라는 뜻의 접두사로, '안으로'라는 뜻의 단어를 만든다.

ex-

halare 숨을 쉬다
ex + halare = exhale 숨을 내쉬다
ex) The yoga instructor told us to exhale slowly.
요가 강사는 우리에게 숨을 천천히 내쉬라고 했다.

- **exit** 나가다, 퇴장하다
- **export** 수출하다   cf) **import** 수입하다
- **exclude** 제외하다   cf) **include** 포함하다
- **extract** ~을 빼내다
- **excavate** 발굴하다
- **explicit** 명시적인, 노골적인   cf) **implicit** 암시적인
- **external** 외부의   cf) **internal** 내부의

in-

put 넣다
in + put = input 투입하다, 입력하다
ex) He quickly inputted the new data into the computer.
그는 서둘러서 새 정보를 컴퓨터에 입력하였다.

- **inhale** 숨을 들이마시다   cf) **exhale** 숨을 내쉬다
- **include** 포함하다   cf) **exclude** 제외하다
- **income** 수입
- **import** 수입하다   cf) **export** 수출하다
- **inbound** 본국행의   cf) **outbound** 외국행의
- **involve** 포함시키다, 관계시키다
- **inseam** 안쪽 솔기

Internal Organs 장기

+ **brain** 뇌

+ **lungs** 폐   /   + **stomach** 위

+ **liver** 간   /   + **heart** 심장

+ **kidneys** 신장

+ **intestines** 창자

+ **bladder** 방광

+ **tonsils** 편도선

VOCA ED

VOCA EDGE SMART_5

Episode

엄마에게,

십대를 어떻게 정의할 수 있나요? 엄마, 엄마는 청소년이었을 때 어땠어요? 순종적이었나요? 반항적이었나요? 전형적인 십대는 어떻다고 생각하세요? 저와 같은 일반적인 십대에 대해 이야기하는 거예요. 십대는 활기가 넘치죠. 우리는 좋아하는 스타를 밖 에서 기다리는 동안 몸이 어는 것도 상관하지 않아요.

우리는 좋아하는 스타의 헤어스타일을 모방하는 것을 좋아해요. 우리는 우리만의 사생활을 원해요. 우리는 사생활이 방해받는 것을 좋아하지 않아요. 우리는 개인 전화를 가지고 있어요. 우리는 스티커로 전화를 장식하는 것을 좋아해요. 엄마, 엄마는 전화로 수다 떠시죠. 우리는 전화로 문자 보내는 것을 더 좋아해요. 우리는 유명인의 이미지를 블로그에 올려요. 우리는 인터넷에 익명의 글을 올리기도 해요. 때로는 무자비한 비판이 문제가 되기도 하지만요. 요즘은 더 많은 십대들이 자신만의 블로그를 가지고 싶어해요.

어떤 블로그는 실질적인 조언을 제공해요. 그런 블로그는 우리가 유행하는 패션을 따라갈 수 있도록 도움을 주기도 해요. 어떤 조언은 효과적인 공부 습관에 관한 것이에요. 문자 메시지를 보내면서 공부에 집중하는 척하는 방법과 같은 조언이죠. 우리가 스트레스를 받을 때 무엇을 하고 싶어하는지 아세요? 우리는 학교 공부를 하는 데 시간을 보내지 않고 친구들과 돌아다니는 것을 더 좋아해요. 떡볶이와 김밥 먹는 걸 좋아해요. 우리는 얼굴에 난 여드름을 짜면서 종종 거울 앞에 서 있죠. 엄마, 엄마가 십대였을 때 엄마도 저와 비슷했나요?

Exercise

A
1. adolescent
2. eager
3. anonymous
4. feast
5. prefer
6. vogue
7. typical
8. imitate
9. decorate
10. interrupt

B
1. rebellion
2. 효과적인
3. define
4. reluctance
5. frozen
6. energetic
7. 공급자
8. obey

C
1. privacy
2. individual
3. harsh
4. ordinary
5. celebrities
6. squeezing
7. stressed
8. concentrate

Episode

당신은 언제 좌절감을 느끼나요? 성적표에 점수가 좋지 않을 때인가요? 친구들로부터 따돌림을 당할 때인가요? 저는 불행이 연속적으로 닥친 적이 있어요. '비가 오면 억수로 퍼붓는다'라는 속담이 생각나요. 아침에 저는 우리 엄마와 심한 말다툼을 했어요. 엄마는 저에게 잠옷을 장롱에 다시 집어넣으라고 강요하셨어요. 저는 싫다고 했어요. 저는 귀를 막고 음악을 계속 들었어요. 엄마는 저에게 화가 많이 나셨어요. 엄마는 제가 못되게 굴었다고 말씀하셨어요. 저는 문을 세게 닫고 집을 나왔어요. 저는 버스를 탔고 버스 안에는 환기가 잘 안되어서 공기가 탁했어요. 나중에 저는 제 행동을 후회했어요. 마음이 불편했어요.

수업 중에 제 휴대 전화가 진동으로 울렸어요. 선생님이 저에게 휴대 전화를 달라고 강요하셨어요. 그리고 나서 선생님은 반 전체 학생들에게 선생님이 제 휴대 전화를 한 달 동안 가지고 계실 거라고 말씀하셨어요. 저는 교통카드를 쓸 수가 없었어요. 교통카드가 제 휴대 전화에 달려 있어서 저는 한동안 집까지 걸어다녀야 했어요. 저는 친구들을 만나기로 되어 있었는데 연락을 할 수가 없어서 우리는 계획을 취소해야 했어요. 이제는 제 휴대 전화가 얼마나 필수적인지 알게 되었어요. 집에서 우리 엄마는 저에게 선생님께 사과하라고 말씀하셨어요. 우리 엄마의 충고를 듣는 게 좋을 것 같아요.

Exercise

A
1. report card
2. successive
3. proverb
4. pour
5. compel
6. misbehave
7. slam
8. ventilation
9. uneasy
10. transportation

B
1. advice
2. apology
3. vibrate
4. 부착
5. furious
6. refusal
7. isolation
8. argue

C
1. report car
2. frustrated
3. successive
4. persisted
5. regretted
6. ventilation
7. transportation
8. indispensable

Episode

브라우니에게,

잘 가, 브라우니. 나는 네가 천국에 있을 거라고 생각해. 브라우니. 너는 사라와 나에게 정말 좋은 친구였어. 나는 네가 얼마나 상냥했는지 기억해. 우리는 너의 털을 보라색으로 염색했어. 너는 운동 신경이 있었어. 판자 위에서 균형을 잡을 수 있었어. 너는 임신했을 때 참치를 좋아했어. 지난달에 너의 강아지 세 마리가 태어났어. 그들은 정말 귀여워. 그 강아지들이 똑같이 생긴 거 알고 있니?

강아지들이 너를 닮았어. 너의 강아지들은 우리에게 축복이야. 그들은 너처럼 모두 순종이야. 우리는 네가 말기 암에 걸렸다는 소식을 듣고 충격을 받았어. 사라는 네가 중환자실로 보내졌다고 나에게 말했어. 나는 마음 아픈 소식을 들었어. 오늘 아침에 우리 모두는 슬퍼했어. 사라는 장례식이 있을 거라고 말했어. 나는 애가를 읽었어. 사라는 하루 종일 울었어. 사라는 절망에 빠져있었어. 나는 사라의 감정에 공감했어.

나는 사라를 위로하려고 했어. 그건 그녀에게는 견딜 수 없는 일이었어. 다른 친구들도 슬픔을 표현했어. 우리는 만장일치로 너를 묻어주기로 동의했어. 우리는 '잘 가, 브라우니'라는 말을 너의 묘비에 새겨 놓았어. 너는 우리 기억 속에 영원히 남아 있을거야.

Exercise

A

1. companion
2. dye
3. balance
4. pregnant
5. resemble
6. pure-bred
7. cancer
8. intensive care unit
9. heartbreaking
10. funeral

B

1. unbearable
2. gracious
3. bear
4. 아주 좋아하다
5. bless
6. cancerous
7. 동일함
8. 유사

C

1. heaven
2. immortal
3. elegy
4. athletic
5. comfort
6. pure-bred
7. unanimously
8. grave

1. define	정의를 내리다
2. persist	지속하다
3. adolescent	청소년
4. furious	격노한
5. obedient	순종적인
6. slam	세게 닫다
7. rebellious	반항적인
8. ventilation	환기
9. energetic	활기가 넘치는
10. temporarily	일시적으로
11. interrupt	방해하다
12. indispensable	필수적인
13. individual	개인적인, 개인
14. companion	친구
15. celebrity	유명인사
16. athletic	운동 신경이 있는
17. anonymous	익명의
18. pregnant	임신한
19. concentrate	집중하다
20. adorable	귀여운
21. reluctant	망설이는
22. identical	똑같은
23. squeeze	쥐어짜다
24. intensive care unit	중환자실
25. frustrated	좌절감을 느낀
26. heartbreaking	마음이 아픈
27. isolated	고립된
28. elegy	애가
29. successive	연속하는
30. condolence	애도

Episode

아빠에게.

아빠, 아빠는 인생이 모순적이라는 데 동의하세요? 어른들이 성숙하다고 확신하세요? 가끔은 저는 아이들이 성숙한 것 같아요. 어른들은 어린 시절을 그리워하는 것처럼 보여요. 아이들처럼 가끔 어른들은 주도권을 차지하려고 싸우곤 해요. 때때로 아이들 과 어른들은 역할을 바꿀 필요가 있어요. 아빠는 아빠 사전에는 싸움이라는 단어는 없다고 말씀하시죠.

아빠는 항상 남자들은 관대하다고 말씀하시죠. 제가 아빠를 오해한 건가요? 생각을 바꾸신 건가요? 어젯밤에 동생과 나는 아빠와 엄마가 연기를 한다고 생각했어요. 두 분 모두 연기하는 데 열중하셨지만, 우리는 차가운 분위기를 느낄 수 있었어요. 우리는 상황이 심각하다는 걸 알았어요. 아빠, 아빠는 괴롭고 걱정스러워 보였어요. 아빠는 전문적인 도움이 필요했어요. 아빠는 필사적 으로 도움을 찾고 있는 것 같았어요. 아이러니하게도 그 도움은 저에게서 나왔어요.

후니는 저에게"두 분이 이혼하실까?"라고 물어봤어요. 저는 아빠가 이런 일을 막을 수 있다고 확신해요. 아빠, 아빠가 먼저 사과하시는 게 어때요? 그냥 엄마가 옳다고 인정하세요. 아빠의 자상한 행동이 엄마를 감동시킬 거예요. 그냥 엄마와 화해하세요. 아빠가 완고하지 않다는 걸 엄마에게 증명해 보이세요. 엄마를 칭찬하고 엄마가 최고의 아내이자 엄마라고 말하세요. 제가 아빠에게 훌륭한 상담자이죠?

Exercise

A
1. contradictory
2. assume
3. childhood
4. dominance
5. misunderstand
6. attitude
7. act
8. atmosphere
9. situation
10. professional

B
1. 상담자
2. 인상적인
3. admit
4. 풍자
5. container
6. dominate
7. 역전
8. maturity

C
1. Compliment
2. stubborn
3. compromise
4. apologize
5. convinced
6. divorce
7. desperately
8. professional

Episode

오늘은 슬프고 기쁜 날이다. 사라의 가족은 미국으로 이민을 갔고 나는 그녀에게서 이메일을 받았다.

보미에게.

보미, 다른 나라로 떠나는 것은 정말 복잡해. 어제 내 애완견인 초코가 예방접종을 받았어. 초코는 면역 예방 주사를 맞았어. 오늘 아침에 우리 가족은 국제 공항으로 갔어. 국제 공항은 국내 공항보다 훨씬 커.

먼저, 우리는 짐을 부쳤어. 그리고 나서 우리는 다음 절차를 밟았어. 공항 직원은 나에게서 초코를 떼어놓으려고 했어. 우리를 떼어놓지 마세요. 나는 그에게 간청했어. 그렇지만 나의 간청은 허사였어. 그는 초코를 화물칸으로 데리고 갔어. 나는 우리가 언제 다시 만날지 궁금했어. 나는 초코와 함께 갈 수 있는지 물어보았지만, 그는 그곳이 제한 구역이라고 말했어. 나는 보안 검색대를 지났어. 저 금속 탐지기는 무엇을 위한 거지? 나는 그 기계가 모든 물건을 검사하는 걸 보았어. 나는 비행기에 올랐어.

기장은 우리가 안전벨트를 매야 한다고 방송했어. 비행기가 올라가기 시작했어. 땅에 있는 집들이 작아지기 시작했어. 42,000피트의 고도에서 날아가는 걸 상상할 수 있니? 갑자기 비행기가 흔들리기 시작했고 나는 무서웠어. 마침내 비행기는 착륙했고 나는 초코를 껴안아 주었어. 18시간의 비행 후에 나는 시차로 인한 피로를 느꼈고 매우 지쳐 있었어. 정말 힘든 날이었어.

Exercise

A
1. emigrate
2. complicated
3. vaccinate
4. immunization
5. international
6. domestic
7. baggage
8. procedure
9. quarantine
10. freight

B
1. plea
2. in vain
3. 안전한
4. detector
5. inspection
6. ascension
7. extremely
8. 길들이다

C
1. extremely
2. embraced
3. threatened
4. altitude
5. shrink
6. fasten
7. boarded
8. restricted

Episode

사라에게,

사라, 나는 지구본을 바라보고 있어. 나는 지도를 너에게 보낼 편지에 함께 넣었어. 오늘 나는 지리학 수업을 들었어. 나는 지구가 5개의 대양과 6개의 대륙으로 이루어져 있다는 걸 배웠어. 사라, 네가 사는 대륙을 찾을 수 있니? 그건 한국에서 몇 인치밖에떨어져 있지 않아. 그렇지? 사람들은 지구가 정사각형이 아니라 타원형이라는 걸 어떻게 발견했을까?

중앙에 있는 적도선이 보이니? 우리가 열대 지방에 살지 않는 건 행운이야. 우리가 덥고 습한 날씨를 얼마나 싫어하는지 나는 기억해. 섭씨 40도의 날씨에서 산다고 상상해봐. 화씨로는 104도가 되는 거야. 우리가 온화한 기후에서 사는 건 운이 좋은 거 아니야? 다행히도 우리는 온대 지역에 살고 있어. 우리는 둘 다 북반구에 살아. 남반구는 지금 여름일 거야. 가로로 된 선이 보이니? 평행한 선 말이야.

손가락을 북쪽으로 움직이면, 북극해를 볼 수 있을 거야. 언젠가 우리는 빙하를 보러 함께 배를 타고 여행하게 될 거야. 그곳에서 거대한 빙하를 볼 수 있어. 우리는 얼음에서 사는 북극곰을 볼 거야. 아니면 우리는 남극에 가서 황제 펭귄을 볼 수 있어. 너는 무엇이 시차와 관련이 있는지 아니? 수직으로 된 선이 보일 거야. 그 선들은 경선이라고 불려. 사라, 네가 사는 도시의 인구가 얼마나 되는지 궁금해. 거기에서는 사람들이 어떤 식물을 경작하니?

Exercise

A
1. population
2. longitude
3. Antarctica
4. Arctic
5. parallel
6. horizontal
7. equivalent
8. mild
9. temperate
10. oval

B
1. 세계적인
2. 열대지방
3. humid
4. glacier
5. vastly
6. related
7. consist of
8. 수평으로

C
1. cultivate
2. longitude
3. vertical
4. inhabiting
5. parallel
6. southern
7. hemisphere
8. zone

1. contradictory	모순적인
2. immunization	예방 주사
3. dominance	우위, 주도권
4. domestic	국내의
5. generous	관대한
6. quarantine	격리시키다
7. attitude	사고방식, 태도
8. freight	화물
9. absorbed	열중한
10. ascend	올라가다
11. atmosphere	분위기
12. altitude	고도
13. situation	상황
14. extremely	매우
15. professional	전문적인
16. geography	지리학
17. desperately	필사적으로
18. equator	적도
19. ironically	반어적으로
20. Celsius	섭씨
21. compromise	화해하다
22. hemisphere	반구
23. complement	칭찬하다
24. horizontal	수평의
25. emigrate	이민 가다
26. parallel	평행한
27. complicated	복잡한
28. Arctic	북극
29. vaccinate	예방접종을 하다
30. Antarctica	남극

Episode

사라에게.
우리 반은 자연 과학 박물관에 갔어. 가장 흥미 있는 것 중 하나는 재생 에너지를 연료로 쓴다는 사실이었어. 우리는 커다란 건물이 태양 에너지로 난방이 되고 있다는 것을 배우고 놀랐어. 우리는 위층으로 가서 진열된 전시품들을 보았어. 우리 조상들의 유해도 포함되어 있었어. 우리는 화석도 보았어. 우리 선생님은 어떤 생물이 화석이 되었다고 설명해 주셨어. 그 화석들은 생명체가 어떻게 생겨났는지 우리에게 보여줄 수 있어. 공룡 뼈도 있었어. 그것들은 거대했어. 사라, 우리가 공룡과 함께 살지 않는 것이 안심이 되지 않니? 우리는 공룡 해골도 보았어. 전시품들은 인간이 어떻게 진화했는지 보여주었어. 인류학자들은 인간이 유인원에서 진화되었다고 믿고 있어. 사라, 우리의 아주 먼 조상이 유인원이었다는 걸 상상할 수 있니?
우리는 천문학 구역으로 옮겨갔어. 그곳에 있던 전시품은 우주가 어떻게 하나의 점에서 시작되었는지 설명해주고 있었어. 그 점이 폭발했어. 그리고 나서 팽창했어. 와, 우리의 우주는 신비로 가득 차 있어. 과학자들은 그렇게 광대한 우주를 어떻게 분석할 수 있는 걸까? 그것은 틀림없이 과학자들에게 만성 두통을 불러일으켰을 거야. 아마도 그들은 생각하기 위해서 진통제를 복용했을 거야. 나는 잠시 동안 고대 그리스 철학자들에 대해 생각해 보았어. 그들은 어떻게 자연 현상을 설명할 수 있었을까? 우리 선생님은 그들이 많은 사색을 했다고 말씀하셨어. 그들은 사물을 관찰했고 가설을 만들었어. 그들은 많은 이론을 만들기도 했어. 휴, 정말 복잡한 과정이야!

Episode

다이어리에게.
우리 삼촌은 대학생이야. 그는 일류 대학에 입학 허가를 받았어. 그 학교는 한국에서 가장 명성 있는 학교야. 입학식 후에 신입생을 위한 오리엔테이션이 있었어. 학생들과 손님들은 강당에 모였어. 그곳은 약 5,000명 정도를 수용할 만큼 컸어. 학장님은 학생들을 칭찬하셨어. 그는 학생들이 얼마나 유능한지 말했어.
그리고 나서 그는 교직원들을 소개했어. 그 후에 그는 학교 생활의 지침을 설명했어. 그리고 나서 학교 신입생 지도 교수님이 무대로 올라오셨어. 그녀는 대학생이 되는 것은 커다란 책임이 따른다고 말씀하셨어. 그녀는 교수님들이 학생들을 어떻게 평가하는지 설명해 주셨고 학기말 리포트가 얼마나 중요한지에 대해 말씀하셨어. 휴, 3년 동안 틀어박혀서 공부를 해야 한다고? 학생들은 그걸 어떻게 견디지? 그들은 나가서 놀 시간을 가질 만하지 않니? 식이 끝난 후에 우리는 삼촌이 살게 될 기숙사로 갔어. 기숙사는 그렇게 호화로워 보이지는 않았어. 1층에는 빨래방이 있었어. 학생들은 그곳에서 세탁을 할 수 있어. 몇 개의 방 문에는 "방해하지 마세요"라는 표시가 붙어 있었어. 그 학교는 남녀공학이었지만, 여학생 기숙사는 분리되어 있었어. 그건 나에게 로미오와 줄리엔이라는 연극을 상기시켰어. 로미오는 줄리엣의 창문을 올려다보면서 그녀에게 세레나데를 불러주었어. 우리 삼촌은 기숙사가 분리되었다는 것에 대해 실망하는 것처럼 보였어. 여학생 기숙사에는 감독관이 있어. 그들은 매일 밤 근무를 교대해. 실망하지 마세요, 삼촌. 이상적인 상대를 발견하면 여학생 기숙사에 사다리를 놓고 올라갈 수 있잖아요.

Exercise

A

1. heat
2. solar
3. organism
4. skull
5. anthropologist
6. ape
7. section
8. chronic
9. painkiller
10. philosopher

B

1. theorize
2. analysis
3. expansion
4. explode
5. 보편적인
6. bony
7. origin
8. 잔존하다

C

1. hypotheses
2. renewable
3. speculated
4. phenomena
5. philosophers
6. mystery
7. apes
8. Anthropologists

Exercise

A

1. college
2. prestigious
3. accommodate
4. praise
5. competent
6. faculty
7. guideline
8. responsibility
9. assess
10. dormitory

B

1. rotation
2. 관용
3. advisor
4. praiseworthy
5. assessment
6. 사치
7. 세탁하다
8. disturbance

C

1. match
2. supervisors
3. disappointed
4. serenaded
5. play
6. co-ed
7. laundromat
8. deserve

Episode

엄마에게,
저는 제가 좋아하는 밴드인 볼케이노에 대한 기사를 읽었어요. 그것은 정말로 저를 화나게 했어요. 그들이 한동안 텔레비전에 나오지 않을 거라고 쓰여 있고 그것이 저의 감정을 자극해요. 몇몇 관계자들은 그 밴드를 검열하기로 결정했어요. 그들은 노래 몇 개의 내용에 문제가 있다고 말했어요. 그들은 그 밴드의 노래가 비교육적이라고 말했어요. 그들은 그 노래들이 학생들을 망칠 거라고 주장해요. 그들은 볼케이노가 범죄자라고 생각하는 것 같아요. 정말 시대에 뒤떨어진 생각이에요! 이걸 결정하는 데 그들은 어떤 기준을 사용했나요? 저는 화가 치밀어요.
의심할 여지 없이 그들은 예술이 무엇인지 몰라요. 엄마, 엄마는 그것이 불합리한 결정이라고 말씀하셨죠. 그들의 노래는 제 마음을 풍성하게 해요. 엄마는 우리가 민주주의 사회에서 산다고 말했어요. 민주주의 사회에서 사람들은 언론의 자유에 대한 권리가 있어요. 그런데 여기에선 무슨 일이 일어나는 거죠? 엄마, 엄마는 제 문자 메시지를 확인하셨어요. 엄마는 그걸 부인할 수 없어요. 후니가 증인이에요. 엄마, 엄마는 자신의 믿음을 배신하실 건가요? 저는 엄마가 객관적이면 좋겠어요. 엄마는 저를 가두려고 하시는 건가요? 엄마가 제 문자 메시지를 확인할 때, 엄마는 저의 언론의 자유를 침해하는 거예요. 죄수들조차도 자신이 원하는 것을 말할 권리가 있어요. 제가 판사라면, 엄마에게 그런 행동을 하지 말라고 명령할 거예요. 엄마는 제 전화를 만질 수 없어요. 이의 있으세요, 엄마?

Exercise

A

1. article
2. arouse
3. content
4. uneducational
5. outdated
6. undoubtedly
7. absurd
8. democracy
9. fresh speech
10. check

B

1. 객관적인
2. judgment
3. betrayal
4. deny
5. in a rage
6. crime
7. censor
8. 파괴

C

1. article
2. stirs
3. contents
4. outdated
5. allowed
6. prisoners
7. confine
8. witness

1. renewable	재생 가능한	
2. assess	평가하다	
3. remains	유해	
4. dormitory	기숙사	
5. organism	생물	
6. luxurious	호화스러운	
7. enormous	거대한	
8. supervisor	감독관	
9. evolve	진화하다	
10. match	어울리는 짝	
11. anthropologist	인류학자	
12. arouse	자극하다	
13. chronic	만성의	
14. criterion	기준, 표준	
15. philosopher	철학자	
16. absurd	불합리한	
17. phenomenon	현상	
18. enrich	풍부하게 하다	
19. hypothesis	가설	
20. democracy	민주주의	
21. prestigious	일류의, 명문의	
22. free speech	언론의 자유	
23. assemble	모이다	
24. objective	객관적인, 목적	
25. accommodate	수용하다	
26. confine	가두다, 제한하다	
27. competent	유능한	
28. prisoner	죄수	
29. faculty	교직원	
30. objection	반대	

Chapter 4 Unit 10

Episode

다이어리에게,

사람들은 왜 산의 정상에 오르려 할까? 나는 최근에 어느 영화배우를 특집으로 한 프로그램을 보았어. 그는 히말라야 산맥에 있는 어떤 산의 정상에 올랐어. 무엇이 그에게 동기를 주었을까? 나는 그의 궁극적인 목표가 무엇이었을까에 대해 생각했어. 아마는 자신의 한계를 시험하고 싶었을지도 몰라. 그것이 나를 궁금하게 만들었어. "우리가 원시 사회에서 살아남을 수 있을까?"

또한 나는 한 남자가 아마존에 있는 어느 부족을 방문했던 쇼를 보았어. 그곳은 미개한 사회였어. 그들은 진짜 미개인 같았어. 그렇지만 그들 사회는 규율이 있었어. 그들은 여전히 원시적인 전통과 의식을 유지했어. 예를 들면, 그들은 악어를 숭배했어. 특별한 날에는 그들의 사제가 의식을 거행했어. 그들은 그 의식이 악령을 몰아낸다고 생각했어. 그들은 매우 미신적인 것처럼 보였어. 나를 놀라게 한 몇 가지 다른 사항은 불이 매우 귀중하다는 것과 그들에게는 벌레가 먹을 수 있는 것이라는 사실이었어. 그들이 그 남자에게 벌레를 먹으라고 요청했을 때, 그는 당황스러워했어. 놀랍게도, 이 사람들은 예리한 감각을 가지고 있으며 사냥할 때 본능을 사용해. 그들은 막대기를 날카롭게 해서 화살을 만들어. 화살을 가지고 그들은 먹을 것을 사냥하고 침략자들로부터 자신을 보호해. 사냥 후에는 큰 축하의식을 갖어. 그들은 음식을 서로에게 나누어 줘. 그들은 종족 전체에서 평등을 유지하려고 노력해. 프로그램의 마지막에, 그 남자는 이 원시적인 생활에 익숙해진 것 같았어. 나는 궁금해. "문명과 미개의 경계는 어디일까?" 둘 사이의 경계선을 표시하는 것은 어려울 것 같아.

Exercise

A
1. peak
2. feature
3. summit
4. limit
5. tribe
6. uncivilized
7. primitive
8. worship
9. priest
10. spirit

B
1. survival
2. orderly
3. equality
4. predator
5. sharpen
6. bewilder
7. 자극하다
8. 마침내

C
1. boundary
2. border
3. distribute
4. instincts
5. superstitious
6. barbarians
7. limits
8. summit

Chapter 4 Unit 11

Episode

유니에게,

유니, 크리스마스 이브에 너는 뭘 할 거니? 동진이는 우리에게 모든 것을 확인하라고 지시했어. 독재자 같지 않아? 그는 항상 고함을 치면서 명령해. 어쨌든 우리는 고아원을 방문하기로 되어 있어. 우리는 그곳에서 자원봉사를 할 거야. 너는 게임, CD, 그리고 몇 가지 장난감도 모아야 해. 그렇지 않으면, 아이들이 실망할 거야. 우리는 또한 음식도 기부받고 있어. 그런 익명의 기부자들이 우리에게 그렇게 많은 물건을 주다니 행운이지. 그들 덕분에 이번 행사는 너무 많은 비용이 들지는 않을 거야. 나는 산타클로스로 변장할 거야. 나는 헐렁한 바지를 입고 가짜 턱수염을 달 거야. 그리고 내 목소리를 과장해서 말할 거야. 유니, 루돌프로 나를 도와 줄 거니? 정호는 코디네이터로 지명되었어. 그가 쇼를 준비할 거야. 그는 전체 과정을 진행할 거야. 그렇지만 누가 그들을 즐겁게 하지? 너는 지수를 추천하는 거니? 그녀의 음악적 기술은 내가 아는 다른 누구보다도 뛰어나다고 생각해. 행사 전에 우리는 그 외에 무엇을 확인해야 하지? 그곳에서 행사가 끝난 후에, 우리는 요양원으로 갈 거야. 노인들이 무엇을 좋아하는지 알고 있니? 우리 할머니는 단것과 우스운 이야기를 정말 좋아하셔. 나는 사람들을 웃게 만드는 재주가 있다는 걸 고백해야겠어. 나는 즉흥적으로 재미있는 이야기를 만들 수 있어. 우리의 유일한 장애물은 우리는 차가 없다는 거야. 엄마한테 지프를 빌려달라고 부탁할 수 있니?

Exercise

A
1. order
2. command
3. volunteer
4. donor
5. disguise
6. loose
7. exaggerate
8. process
9. entertain
10. recommend

B
1. 명령하다
2. orphanage
3. collection
4. dissatisfy
5. donation
6. 값비싼
7. 조수
8. humorous

C
1. lend
2. obstacle
3. improvise
4. confess
5. senior citizens
6. nursing home
7. confirm
8. recommend

Chapter 4 Unit 12

REVIEW TEST Unit 10~ Unit 12

Episode

사라는 잘 적응하는 것 같다. 여기 그녀에게서 온 이메일이 있다.

보미에게.

안녕, 보미. 우리 지역사회는 특별한 행사를 열고 있어. 1년에 두 번 있는 행사야. 시 의회가 그 행사를 후원해. 나는 다양한 민족의 사람들을 만났어. 마지막에 축구 경기 결승전과 파티가 열렸어. 전통적으로 라이온스와 베어스 두 팀 사이에 격렬한 경쟁이 있어. 경기 전에 한 남자가 시작을 알렸어. 그는 축구공 모양의 트로피에 맥주를 붓기도 했어. 나는 마치 내가 광고를 보는 것같은 느낌이 들었어. 양팀의 선수들은 선서를 했어. 그들은 진지해 보였어. 그들은 엄숙해 보였어. 그들은 나에게 전사를 상기시켰어. 그들은 각 지역사회의 대표단으로 거기에 있었어. 우리 팀 선수인 카를로스는 두 골을 넣어서 점수를 올렸어. 그의 경기는 대항할 수 없는 것이었어. 그의 기술은 정교했어. 그가 경기하는 것을 보면서 사람들은 경외심을 가졌어. 사람들은 그가 마치 전설적인 축구 선수인 것처럼 그를 칭송했어. 그의 적들은 그와는 상대할 수가 없었어. 후반전에 카를로스는 앞서가면서 우수한 경기를 계속했어. 그는 또 한 골을 넣었고 사람들은 환호했어. 관중들은 압도되었어. 게임이 끝난 후에 다국적 파티가 열렸어. 사람들은 다양한 음식을 준비했어. 나는 다양한 악센트로 영어를 말하는 사람들을 만날 수 있었어. 그리고 나는 부모님을 위해 통역했어.

Exercise

A

1. community
2. biannual
3. sponsor
4. oath
5. solemn
6. warrior
7. score
8. unmatchable
9. sophisticated
10. opponent

B

1. ethnicity
2. 완성시키다
3. rivalry
4. shaped
5. 경외하여
6. legend
7. 나아가다
8. variety

C

1. translated
2. accents
3. multinational
4. spectators
5. applauded
6. opponents
7. sophisticated
8. unmatchable

1. motivate	동기부여하다	
2. entertain	즐겁게 하다	
3. ultimate	궁극적인	
4. confirm	확인하다	
5. uncivilized	미개한	
6. nursing home	양로원	
7. barbarian	미개인, 야만인	
8. senior citizen	노인	
9. primitive	원시적인, 초기의	
10. improvise	즉흥적으로 만들다	
11. worship	숭배, 예배	
12. community	지역사회	
13. superstitious	미신적인	
14. biannual	1년에 두 번의	
15. bewildered	당황한	
16. ethnic	민족의	
17. instinct	예리한	
18. commencement	개회식	
19. boundary	경계선	
20. commercial	상업광고	
21. orphanage	고아원	
22. solemn	엄숙한	
23. dissatisfied	불만스러운	
24. sophisticated	정교한	
25. disguise	변장하다	
26. opponent	적수, 상대	
27. exaggerate	과장하다	
28. spectator	관중	
29. designate	지명하다	
30. multinational	다국적의	

Episode

보미 : 엄마, 이 음악은 뭐예요? 정말 단조롭네요. 경쾌한 음악을 들으시는 게 어때요?

엄마 : 보미, 이건 명상 음악이야. 정신 건강에 좋아. 마음을 정화하는 데에도 도움이 된단다.

보미 : 엄마, 엄마는 불교의 수도사가 아니잖아요.

엄마 : 너는 명상의 진정한 가치를 모르는구나.

보미 : 엄마는 명상이 스트레스를 줄이는 데 효과가 있다고 생각하세요? 스트레스 해소에는 힙합 음악이 더 나은 선택이에요.

우리 엄마는 요가 클래스에 등록하셨다. 명상 음악을 듣는 것이 엄마의 일과 중 하나이다. 엄마는 요가가 우리에게 이롭다고 말씀하신다. 엄마는 요가가 건강에 이롭다는 걸 강조하신다. 엄마는 요가 클래스를 시작하시기 전에는 궤양이 있으셨는데, 지금은 괜찮으시다. 이것 때문에 나는 비슷한 것을 생각하게 되었다. 엄마는 차가 치료 효과가 있다고 말씀하신 적이 있다. 요즘 엄마는 요가를 하면서 건강을 유지하신다. 우리 엄마는 요가가 사람을 가르치는 데 좋다고 말씀하신다. 엄마는 또한 요가가 인생에 대한 통찰력을 주고 우리의 감정을 통제하는 데 도움을 준다고 말씀하신다. 엄마는 요가에 정통한 사람들을 정말 동경하신다. 오늘 아침에 엄마는 몇 가지 기본 자세를 시범을 보이셨다. 엄마는 나보고 다리를 뻗어보라고 시키기도 하셨다.

보미 : 아야, 이건 고문이에요. 엄마, 저는 이 자세를 유지할 수 없어요. 제 어깨를 누르지 마세요.

엄마 : 보미, 좀 더 끈기가 있어야겠구나. 이 운동은 사람의 장기를 강화하는 데 효과가 있어.

보미 : 알았어요, 엄마. 해보겠지만 제 몸이 너무 뻣뻣해요.

Exercise

A
1. option
2. routine
3. ulcer
4. recall
5. enlighten
6. press
7. monotonous
8. lively
9. Buddhist
10. register

B
1. 근육통이 경직되다
2. healing
3. emotional
4. 지력
5. 순수한
6. valuable
7. 경감
8. emphasize

C
1. strengthening
2. tenacity
3. press
4. maintain
5. torture
6. stretch
7. recall
8. admires

Episode

다이어리에게,

오늘 우리는 연극 "한 여름밤의 꿈"의 예행연습을 했어. 선배들은 나에게 어려운 일을 주었어. 보미, 이 장비를 아래층으로 옮겨줄래? 선배들은 정신이 나간 것일까? 내가 어떻게 그렇게 무거운 걸 옮길 수 있지? 그렇지만 나는 거절할 수 없어. 선배의 명령을 따르는 것이 의무거든. 나는 안 된다고 말할 권리가 없어. 그들은 왜 그렇게 인정이 없을까? 사려 깊은 선배들이 왜 이런 태도를 보이는 걸까? 공연 바로 전에, 우리는 특별 훈련을 받아. 후배들과 선배들 사이에 긴장감이 감돌지. 모든 선배들은 매우 엄해지고 우리의 관계는 고용인과 고용주의 관계와 같이 되어가고 있어. 보통 후배들은 선배들의 회의실에 들어갈 수 없어, 회의실은 회사의 중역을 위한 방과 같은 거야. 그 방은 선배들에게만 개방되어 있어. 그들은 선후배 사이에 계급을 만드는 거야. 선배들은 모든 것을 감시해. 우리는 무언가를 하기 위해서는 허락을 받아야 해. 우리는 급여나 휴가를 달라고 요구할 수 없어. 아버지 출산 휴가나 어머니 출산 휴가는 없어. 우리는 완전히 노예가 되어가고 있어. 보미, 바닥을 청소해. 빨리 청소해. 좋아, 보미, 융통성을 발휘해 봐. 나는 혼잣말을 했어. 너는 내 반응이 너무 수동적이라고 생각할지도 몰라. 나는 이 문제에 대해 마음 속에 갈등이 있는 게 사실이야. 선배들은 그것이 더 나은 공연을 위한 것이라고 말하면서 항상 자신들의 행동을 정당화해. 2년 후에 나도 같은 특권을 갖게 되겠지. 그래서 나는 나의 미래에 대해 그렇게 비관적이지 않아.

Exercise

A
1. employer
2. inconsiderate
3. monitor
4. flexible
5. reject
6. exclusively
7. acuum
8. equipment
9. justify
10. thoughtful

B
1. 예행연습
2. insanity
3. trainee
4. 긴장한
5. 계급제의
6. permission
7. passivity
8. 특권

C
1. obligatory
2. juniors
3. executives
4. maternity leave
5. literally
6. conflict
7. privilege
8. pessimistic

Episode

보미 : 후니, 봐. 네 카드가 사방에 널려 있어. 카드 좀 버려.
후니 : 걱정하지 마. 가장 좋은 폐기 방법을 알고 있어. 보미, 날 그렇게 의심스러운 눈초리로 쳐다보지 마.

두 달 동안, 후니는 매일 이상한 카드를 샀어. 후니는 마치 이 쓸모없는 것들에 사로잡힌 것 같았어. 내가 카드에 대해서 물어보면 후니는 나를 보고 그냥 웃기만 했어. 이 카드를 모으는 목적이 뭐야? 그러면 후니는 자신의 계획을 나에게 말해주었어. 후니는 의기양양하게 가방에서 비디오 게임을 꺼냈어. 후니는 자신의 카드를 친구인 브라이언의 새 비디오 게임과 바꿨어. 와, 후니는 경제가 어떻게 움직이는지 알고 있는 것 같아. 후니는 어떻게 이익을 남길 수 있을지를 알아. 후니는 이미 기본적인 이론을 습득하고 있어. 내 말은, 후니가 물물교환 시스템이 어떻게 돌아가는지 안다는 거야. 후니, 브라이언이 마음을 바꾸면 어떻게 할 거니? 후니는 글로 쓴 서류를 나에게 보여주었어. 그들은 계약서에 서명을 했다고 말했어. 계약서에는 특정 조건이 언급되어 있어. 예를 들면, 계약은 9월 21일까지 유효하다. 그리고 나서 계약은 만기가 된다. 후니는 틀림없이 훌륭한 협상가야. 거래를 너무 잘 하는 것 같아. 후니는 브라이언이 이런 낡은 카드와 새 비디오 게임을 바꿀 수 있도록 어떻게 설득했을까? 후니는 그렇게 이익이 많이 남는 거래를 어떻게 성사시켰을까? 후니는 자신이 브라이언에게 몇 가지 카드 샘플을 보여주었고 브라이언이 그걸 정말 좋아했다고 말했어. 후니의 자택 학습은 정말 잘 되어가고 있어. 우리 아빠는 후니에게 금전출납부를 쓰라고 말씀하셨어. 아빠는 후니에게 수입과 지출의 의미를 가르쳐주셨어. 후니는 이미 돈 쓰는 방법을 알고 있어.

Exercise

A

1. disposal
2. purchase
3. grin
4. purpose
5. divulge
6. triumphantly
7. brand-new
8. surplus
9. barter
10. contract

B

1. statement
2. 회계사
3. validate
4. economic
5. expire
6. acquire
7. 이익이 되는
8. 강박관념

C

1. privacy
2. individual
3. harsh
4. ordinary
5. celebrities
6. squeezing
7. stressed
8. concentrate

1. monotonous		단조로운
2. executive		중역
3. meditation		명상
4. hierarchy		계급제
5. purify		정화하다
6. maternity leave		출산 휴가
7. routine		일과
8. flexible		융통성이 있는
9. emphasize		강조하다
10. pessimistic		비관적인
11. ulcer		궤양
12. disposal		폐기
13. enlighten		가르치다
14. suspicious		의심스러운
15. insight		통찰력
16. obsess		사로잡다
17. demonstrate		시범을 보이다
18. divulge		누설하다
19. tenacity		끈기
20. triumphantly		의기양양해서
21. rehearsal		예행연습
22. surplus		흑자
23. equipment		장비
24. negotiator		협상가
25. obligatory		의무적인
26. convince		설득하다
27. inconsiderate		인정 없는
28. homeschooling		자택 학습
29. thoughtful		사려 깊은
30. expenditure		지출

Episode

보미: 엄마, 할머니 치료하는 의사를 만나실 거예요? 그리고 후니의
　　담당의사도 만나실 거죠, 그렇죠?
엄마: 아니, 나와 함께 한의원에 갈 거야.
보미: 한의사를 말씀하시는 거예요? 후니는 발목이 삐었고 할머니는
　　혈압이 높으시잖아요. 침술을 생각하시는 건가요?
엄마: 물론이야. 그게 혈액순환에 좋거든.

엄마는 항상 침술이 혈액 순환을 원활하게 한다고 말씀하신다. 엄마
는 침술에 중독되신 것 같다. 언젠가 내가 식중독에 걸렸을 때. 엄마
는 나를 갑자기 한의원에 데려가셨다. 한의원에서 의사는 내 맥박을
짚었다. 그리고 나서 상상할 수 있어? 나는 검정색 액체를 마셔야 했
다. 첫눈에도 그건 맛이 쓸 것 같았다. 나는 정말 마시고 싶지 않았지
만, 그건 강제적이었다. 오늘은 후니가 같은 경험을 할 것이다. 엄마
는 주사를 무서워하는 것은 유전이라고 하신다. 엄마는 아빠가 주사
에 대한 공포증이 있어서 후니와 나도 그렇다고 말씀하신다. 그렇
지만 엄마가 어떻게 후니를 안심시킬 수 있을까? 후니가 진료실에 들
어가지 않으려고 하지 않을까? 후니는 미친 듯이 울어댈 것이다. 간
호사는 후니를 단단히 붙들 것이고 후니는 인질이 되겠지. 불쌍한 내
동생. 엄마는 잔인해요. 그것이 아동 학대라고 생각하지 않으세
요? 제 말이 맞다고 인정하시는 것이 어떠세요?

Exercise

A

1. physician
2. pediatrician
3. blood pressure
4. acupuncture
5. stimulate
6. pulse
7. imagine
8. glance
9. compulsory
10. hostage

B

1. abusive
2. frantic
3. soothe
4. phobia
5. orient
6. herb
7. 중독
8. 독

C

1. pulse
2. acknowledge
3. inhumane
4. hesitate
5. sprained
6. experience
7. liquid
8. circulation

Episode

사라에게,
사라, 너의 친구는 이제 괜찮니? 나는 방울뱀이 그렇게 독이 있는 줄
몰랐어. 너의 선생님이 신속한 조치를 취한 건 현명한 행동이었어.
그렇지 않았으면 네 친구는 몸이 마비되었을 수도 있었어. 유독한 상
태에 빠질 수도 있었어. 사라, 사막에서 뱀에게 물리는 사상자들이
많이 있어? 여행객들은 사막을 지날 때 조심해야만 해. 그곳에 사는
뱀은 타고난 위장술을 가지고 있어. 사람들은 뱀과 모래를 거의 구별
할 수 없어. 그 생물학자에 대한 너의 비디오는 나를 놀라게 했어. 그
는 그렇게 치명적인 뱀을 어떻게 잡을 수 있었을까? 그는 뱀을 다루
면서 동시에 뱀에 대해 설명하기도 했어. 그는 뱀의 독이 자신의 신
경계를 해칠 수도 있다는 사실을 무시하는 것처럼 보였어. 아니면 그
는 해독제를 들고 다녔나? 살아남기 위해서 우리는 위급한 상황에
대처할 수 있어야 해. 그런 상황은 우리에게 갑자기 오니까. 오늘은
모든 학생들이 인체 모형을 놓고 실험했어. 우리는 구조팀이 되었어.
사라, 어린 소년이 작은 레고 블록을 삼켰다고 상상해봐. 그의 호흡
기관이 제대로 기능을 다 하지 못하게 될 거야. 그 소년이 응급실로
보내어지기 전에 뭔가 조치를 취해야 해. 그렇지 않으면 그 소년은
질식할 거야. 우리 선생님은 우리에게 몇 가지 필요한 기술을 시범
보이셨어. 그는 사람의 기도를 막고 있는 것을 제거하는 방법을 가르
쳐주셨어. 그는 또한 숨을 들이쉬는 방법도 보여주셨어. 우리는 인형
을 누르는 것도 배웠어. "이봐, 배가 아니라 가슴을 눌러" 선생님은
나에게 말씀하셨어. 인체 모형을 가지고 노는 것은 전혀 재미가 없었
지만, 나는 이 가르침을 기억할 거야. 가까운 미래에 내가 그 방법들
을 사용하게 될지 누가 알겠어?

Exercise

A

1. critical
2. casualty
3. camouflage
4. lethal
5. simultaneously
6. nervous system
7. antidote
8. unexpectedly
9. experiment
10. swallow

B

1. instruction
2. elimination
3. 본질
4. rescuer
5. cope with
6. biologist
7. cautious
8. 신속하게

C

1. in mind
2. abdomen
3. inhale
4. suffocate
5. emergency
6. respiratory
7. unexpectedly
8. antidote

Episode

웃음이 얼마나 대단한지 아니? 웃음은 기적과 같은 효과가 있고 인생에 미치는 영향은 대단해. 하하하… 우리 할머니는 운동과 웃음을 결합시킨 치료를 두 달 동안 받으셨어. 한때 할머니가 우울증에 시달렸다는 걸 믿을 수 있니? 작년에 할머니의 친한 친구 분이 알츠하이머병이라는 진단을 받으셨어. 그 소식을 듣고 할머니는 입맛을 잃으셨어. 할머니는 심지어 쓰러지셨어. 의사는 할머니의 골밀도가 낮아지고 있다고 말했어. 할머니는 청력도 악화되고 있다고 말씀하셨어. 할머니는 자신이 늙고 있다고 결론 내리셨어. 할머니는 자신이 더 이상 지적인 것 같지 않다고 말씀하셨어. 할머니는 더 이상 사람들과 말하려고 하지 않으셨어. 그렇지만 지금은 아무것도 할머니를 막을 수 없어. 할머니는 활기차시고 항상 우리를 웃게 하셔. 할머니는 고기보다는 야채를 더 많이 드시려고 하셔.
"내 노화방지 크림이 어디에 있니?" "내 운동복은 어디에 있니?" "나에게 카페인이 들어 있지 않은 음료수를 줄래?" 말씀하셔. 이제 우리 가족 모두는 웃음이 항체를 만들어 낸다는 걸 확실히 알아. 할머니의 수명은 분명히 연장되었을 거야. 주름조차도 없어진 것 같아. 할머니는 얼굴에 노화방지 크림을 바를 필요조차 없으셔. 분명히 웃음은 최고의 약이야. 더군다나 전염성이 있어. 그래서 웃음은 우리에게 영향을 미치고 전염병처럼 퍼져. 네가 웃는데 누가 따라 웃지 않겠어?

Exercise

A

1. impact
2. collapse
3. deteriorate
4. ntellectual
5. anti-aging
6. sweatsuit
7. decaffeinated
8. antibody
9. life expectancy
10. wrinkle

B

1. infectious
2. 명백한
3. motive
4. 활기에 찬
5. interact
6. aging
7. 밀도
8. laugh

C

1. miracle
2. combining
3. depression
4. diagnosed
5. appetite
6. deteriorating
7. impede
8. consume

1. physician	내과의사
2. biologist	생물학자
3. pediatrician	소아과 의사
4. simultaneously	동시에
5. oriental	동양의
6. nervous system	신경계
7. sprained	접지른
8. swallow	삼키다
9. blood pressure	혈압
10. respiratory	호흡의
11. acupuncture	침술
12. suffocate	질식하다
13. circulation	순환
14. essential	필요한
15. poisoning	중독
16. eliminate	제거하다
17. abruptly	갑작스럽게
18. abdomen	복부
19. compulsory	강제적인
20. keep in mind	기억해 두다
21. hereditary	유전성의
22. depression	우울증
23. frantically	미친 듯이
24. impede	방해하다
25. paralyzed	마비된
26. sweat suit	운동복
27. camouflage	위장, 위장 수단
28. decaffeinated	카페인이 없는
29. distinguish	구별하다
30. life expectancy	평균 수명

어휘집의 놀라운 진화!!
국내 최초 Storytelling VOCA가 떴다!

Reading, Listening, Conversation까지
영역별 연계학습이 가능한 획기적인 교재!

- 초 · 중등 · 수능 필수 어휘 5,800개 총망라
- 개별 단어의 나열이 아닌, 10대의 일상생활 속 이야기가 스토리라인으로 구성
- 주제별 12개 Chapter와 그 안에 100여 개의 Episode를 수록
- 총 12개의 주제별 Chapter와 각 Chapter당 2~4개의 Unit(지문) 구성

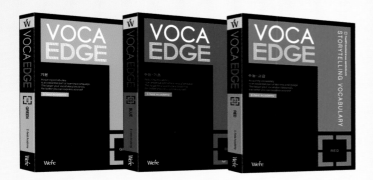

STORYTELLING VOCABULARY
VOCA EDGE

E-field Academy 지음 | 신국판 (150x220)
Green 276면 | 값 **10,000원**
Blue 304면 • Red 428면 | 각 값 **11,000원**
부록: 어휘와 Episode 음원, Dictation Sheet 제공

6단계로 필수 어휘 정복!
독해+리스닝+어휘 학습을 한번에!

▶ VOCA EDGE의 우수한 컨텐츠에 학습자 편의를 보강한 교습용 교재
▶ 초급에서 고급까지 체계적인 어휘 훈련이 가능한 총 6단계 구성

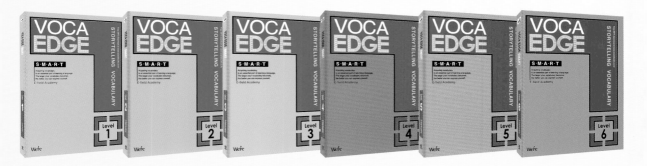

STORYTELLING VOCABULARY
VOCA EDGE SMART

E-field Academy 지음 | 4X6배판
1 · 2 · 3 · 4 각 권 값 **8,500원**
5 · 6 각 권 값 **9,500원**
부록: 학습자료 CD (Unit별 지문&MP3, 연습문제 파일)

VOCA EDGE SMART
Free MP3 download at www.wearebooks.co.kr

□ 레벨별 구성표

난이도	어휘 수	대상	특징
Level 1	278	중등 1 ~ 중등 2	14개의 에피소드 / 기본 필수어휘 + 파생어
Level 2	371	중등 2 ~ 중등 3	18개의 에피소드 / 기본 필수어휘 + 파생어
Level 3	427	중등 3 ~ 고등 1	18개의 에피소드 / 기본 필수어휘 + 파생어 + 숙어
Level 4	438	고등 1 ~ 고등 2	18개의 에피소드 / 기본 필수어휘 + 파생어 + 숙어
Level 5	497	고등 2 ~ 고등 3	18개의 에피소드 / 기본 필수어휘 + Phrasal verb + 영영 뜻풀이
Level 6	614	고3 (수능 · 고급)	22개의 에피소드 / 기본 필수어휘 + Phrasal verb + 영영 뜻풀이

□ VOCA EDGE SMART SERIES

The VOCA EDGE SMART series will help you simultaneously enlarge your vocabulary and improve your English.

This series uses an intergrated approach to learning English.

Listening, reading, writing and comprehension are all covered in this series.

One of the key features of this series is that it revolves around the daily lives of several characters and the challenges they face in growing up. By reading each episode, students will learn the natual and functional use of English vocabulary.

We are confident that the VOCA EDGE SMART series can help you make a dramatic improvement in your English ability.

9,500 won

54740

9 788993 258837

ISBN 978-89-93258-83-7
ISBN 978-89-93258-85-1 (세트)

We're